Keyboarding
with
WordPerfect
5.1

Jean Gonzalez & Ric Williams

Mitchell McGRAW-HILL
New York St. Louis San Francisco Auckland Bogotá Caracas
Hamburg Lisbon London Madrid Mexico Milan Montreal
New Delhi Oklahoma City Paris San Juan São Paulo Singapore
Sydney Tokyo Toronto Watsonville

Mitchell **McGraw-Hill**
55 Penny Lane
Watsonville, CA 95076

Keyboarding with WordPerfect 5.1

1 2 3 4 5 6 7 8 9 0 SEM SEM 9 0 9 8 7 6 5 4 3 2 1

P/N 046241-0

ORDER INFORMATION:
ISBN 0-07-046241-0

Sponsoring editor: James Hill
Production manager: Betty Drury
Series concept and creation: Susan Nelle, BMR
Production services by BMR
Copy edit: Barbara Milligan
Cover and text design: Paul Quin
Desktop production: Patricia Douglass and Curtis Philips
Development management: Christine Hunsicker
Project management: Terrence O'Donnell
Printer: Semline, Inc.

Library of Congress Catalog Card No. 90-83389

Contents

CHAPTER **3**

Keyboarding the Alphabet and Moving the Cursor

Preface

Keyboarding means entering text and numbers into a computer by using a keyboard. While typewriting produces a document on paper, keyboarding produces a document that you can electronically manipulate and store in the computer.

Until the past few years, using a keyboard was a specialized skill for writers, clerks, and secretaries. With microcomputers, however, keyboarding has become a necessary skill for any professional who uses a computer to help perform a task or make a decision. No matter what your profession—whether you are a stockbroker, professor, salesperson, marketing executive, banker, construction contractor, financial analyst, or human resource specialist—keyboarding can help you do your work more quickly and easily.

One of the challenges for busy professionals or students is learning how to keyboard without sacrificing time away from responsibilities. One solution is to present keyboarding in the same computer environment in which professionals often work—WordPerfect 5.1. By using WordPerfect 5.1 to gain keyboarding skills, you can acquire two skills at the same time: (1) you learn how to operate a keyboard with proficiency, and (2) you become familiar with the most popular business word processor on the market.

Using this book, you can learn in as few as 20 hours how to keyboard text at about 25 words per minute (wpm). By spending additional time, you can learn how to:

1. Increase your keyboarding speed.
2. Use basic WordPerfect 5.1 word processing functions, such as underlining, bolding, centering, and indenting.
3. Create a variety of documents, including letters, macro code, reports, and resumes.
4. Key statistical material using both top-row and numeric keypad fingering.
5. Learn the vocabulary common to WordPerfect 5.1.

You can use this book either to develop basic keyboarding skills or to become adept at keyboarding. You can use it to create simple letters or to format more complex reports.

How To Use This Book

The text is self-instructional; you can use it either on your own or in a classroom. To help you schedule your time and learn only the skills that meet your needs, the book is divided into seven chapters, as shown in Table 1.

- Chapter 1 introduces the microcomputer and the WordPerfect 5.1 concepts that you need to know in order to complete the lessons.
- Chapters 2 and 3 show how to key the alphabet with WordPerfect 5.1 using appropriate fingering.
- Chapters 4 and 5 present intermediate skills, such as how to use WordPerfect 5.1 to set tabs, change line spacing, and keyboard the number and symbol keys.
- Chapters 6 and 7 provide exercises to help you apply what you learned in previous chapters and to help you create documents.

By completing the first three chapters, you will be able to perform basic tasks such as keyboarding at a moderate speed and saving and printing lessons. By completing the intermediate chapters, you will be able to use function keys to format text. By completing all the chapters, you will be able to operate WordPerfect 5.1 in almost any business environment.

Acknowledgements

A tremendous team of people have helped to create this book. The authors would like to thank the editorial and production staffs at Business Media Resources for their consistent support and encouragement; in particular, Susan Nelle, Matthew Lusher, Jane Granoff, Christine Hunsicker, Melanie Field, and Terrence O'Donnell. The authors would also like to thank Yoshiko Izumi for her willing assistance.

We are indebted to the book *Exhibits for the Small Museum: A Handbook*, by Arminta Neal, for its discussion on creating display exhibits. Also, *Exhibit Methods*, by Jefferson Warren, proved indispensable for providing background on exhibit techniques. We would especially like to thank Alan Simpson for his excellent WordPerfect 5.1 reference book, *Mastering WordPerfect 5.1*, which was always a useful technical resource.

TABLE I

Skill Level	Chapter	Topic
Basic	1	Using WordPerfect 5.1
	2	The Alphabet
	3	The Alphabet
Intermediate	4	WordPerfect 5.1 Function Keys
	5	Numbers, Symbols, Numeric Keypad
Proficiency	6	Practicing Keystrokes
	7	Creating Documents

1

How to Use WordPerfect 5.1

Lesson 1   What is a Microcomputer Word Processor?

Personal computers have changed the production of reports, correspondence, and manuscripts. Tasks that once took hours can now take minutes.

Using a *microcomputer* and a *word processing application program*, such as WordPerfect 5.1, you can delete, insert, or move text on the screen. Regardless of how many drafts of a memo or letter you make, you usually have to keyboard the text only once.

The first thing you should know when working with a microcomputer is that the computer is not one machine but several devices working together. Let's look at these devices more closely.

The Five Elements of a Microcomputer

A microcomputer system is a group of devices, called *hardware*, that allow you to do a task. As shown in Figure 1.1, these devices include (1) the keyboard, (2) the central processing unit (CPU), (3) the display, (4) the printer, and (5) storage.

What Is a Keyboard?

A *computer keyboard* is similar to an ordinary typewriter keyboard with the exception that it has a number of extra keys (see Figure 1.2). The most important of these are the *function keys*, which are labeled F1 through F12 (or sometimes F1 through F10). WordPerfect 5.1 is designed so that you can use these extra keys to command the program.

FIGURE I.I *A microcomputer consists of (1) the keyboard, (2) the central processing unit (CPU), (3) the display monitor, (4) the printer, and (5) storage.*

You should be aware that there are two basic kinds of keyboards: *regular* and *enhanced*. The regular keyboard has fewer keys than the enhanced and places the function keys on the left side of the keyboard. On enhanced keyboards, the function keys are at the top of the keyboard.

The keyboard alone, though, cannot manipulate text. To perform tasks, you need the central processing unit.

FIGURE 1.2 *The most common computer keyboards are the regular and the enhanced keyboards.*

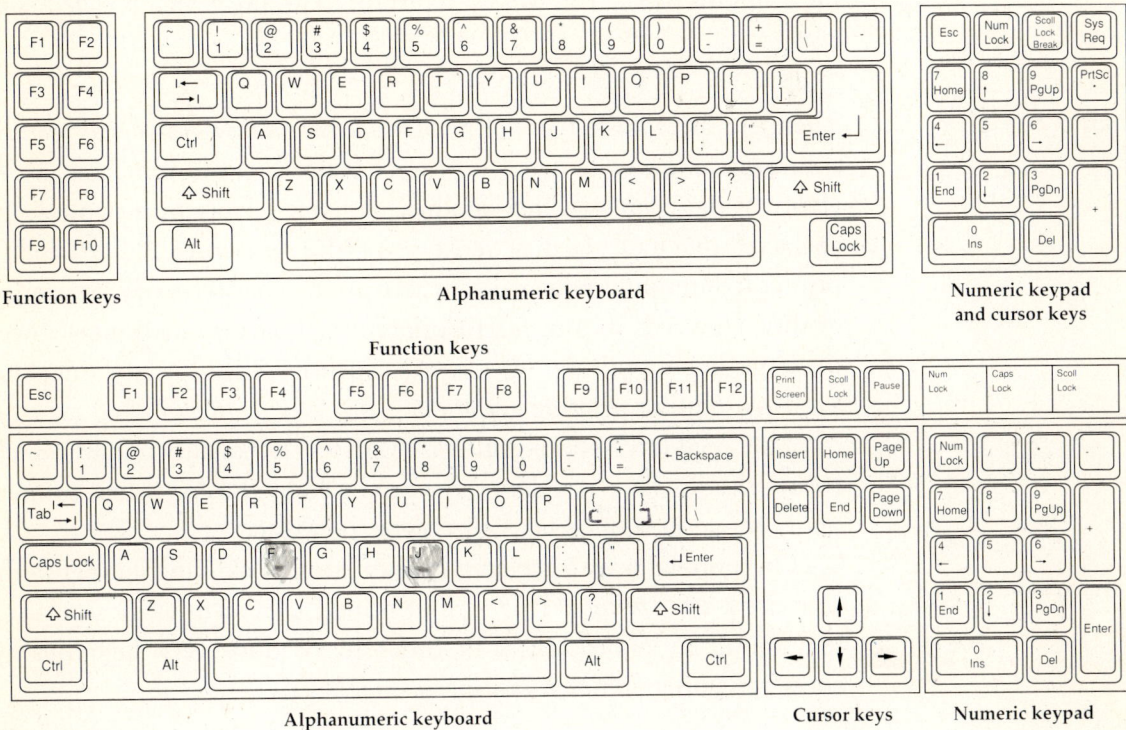

Function keys   Alphanumeric keyboard   Numeric keypad and cursor keys

Function keys

Alphanumeric keyboard   Cursor keys   Numeric keypad

What Is a Central Processing Unit?

Similar to the engine in a car, the *central processing unit* (CPU) is the electronic circuitry that enables the computer to carry out commands. The CPU sends and receives text and other information in and out of the computer's *memory*, called RAM, which is short for *random access memory*.

Different computers have different amounts of memory. Generally, the more RAM that is in the CPU, the more complex are the tasks that the computer can perform. Memory is measured in electronic units called *bytes*. For example, microcomputers can contain anywhere from 640 thousand to several million bytes of memory. To help refer to such large numbers, most people use the letter K (*kilobytes*) to mean one thousand bytes and the letters MB (*megabytes*) to mean millions of bytes; for example, a CPU can contain 640K or four MBs of RAM.

What Is a Display?

After you have keyboarded the document into the CPU, the computer needs a way to tell you what it is doing. The most common way for the computer to communicate with you is with a *display monitor*. The display monitor, which looks similar to a TV screen, allows you to see your keyboarded text, called *soft copy*.

When you have finished working with the text, you are ready to print the result on paper. You will use a printer to produce what is called *hard copy*.

What Is a Printer?

There are three basic types of printers: *letter quality*, *near-letter quality*, and *draft quality*. The major difference between these printers is in the clarity of the print that they produce. A letter-quality printer produces characters that look like they were typed with a typewriter. A draft-quality printer (commonly called a dot-matrix printer) has relatively poor print quality. However, the dot-matrix printer has three major advantages over the letter-quality printer: (1) it is less expensive, (2) it prints faster, and (3) it is useful for printing graphics.

The "medium" type of printer is the near-letter quality printer, which creates clearer characters than those produced by the dot-matrix printer, but is not good enough for formal correspondence.

One popular way to get letter-quality print quickly and inexpensively is to use a *laser printer*. This type of printer uses technology similar to that found in photocopiers in order to produce very high quality characters and graphics at fast speed.

What Is Storage?

Once you have printed a document, you need a way to store it electronically so that you can use it later if necessary. The two most popular ways to store text are with floppy disks and with hard disks.

A *floppy disk* is a square piece of plastic, either 3.5" or 5.25" wide, that encases a round magnetic disk. As a rule of thumb, the smaller the disk, the more data it can hold; 3.5" disks can store up to 1.4 megabytes of data, while 5.25" disks store up to 1.2 megabytes. In practical terms, these disks can hold about 600 pages of text.

A more convenient form of storage is the hard disk. Although not much larger than a floppy disk, a hard disk can contain between 10 and 150 megabytes of data, or about 5,000 to 75,000 pages of text. While this sounds like a lot of storage space, you might be surprised at how quickly you can fill it up. In addition to your document, you also need to store the programs that run the machine and manipulate the text, as discussed in the next section.

Software to Manipulate Text

In order to operate, computers need instructions, called *software*, that tell the hardware what to do. Two kinds of software are operating system software and application software, such as WordPerfect 5.1.

The Disk Operating System

When you turn on a computer, nothing will happen unless you have *operating system software.* A common operating system software is called DOS, which stands for Disk Operating System. DOS, like other operating systems, tells the computer what to do—how to send data to and from storage, printers, display monitors, and the CPU.

The Final Element: The WordPerfect 5.1 Application Software

The last element of a microcomputer word processor is the *application software,* which you use to complete a task. Often, the application is the only software that you see when you use a microcomputer. Word processing application software, such as WordPerfect 5.1, allows you to keyboard text and then format it in different ways by changing the line spacing, setting new tabs, and so on.

By combining hardware (such as the keyboard, CPU, display monitor, printer, and storage) with software (such as WordPerfect 5.1), you can create a microcomputer word processing system that helps you to create documents and complete your work.

Before you actually begin keyboarding, we suggest that you take a few moments to make sure that your work environment is as comfortable and safe as possible.

Creating an Ergonomic Environment

You can increase your keyboarding speed and accuracy, as well as enhance the quality of your work, by designing an *ergonomic* work environment. Ergonomics is the science of creating work areas that allow you to do tasks effectively and safely. Consider the care that the manufacturers of luxury cars take as they design the interiors of their cars. As you know, a well-designed car interior can make it easy and relaxing to drive for long periods of time. A well-designed word processing environment can help you to stay alert while working the long hours that are often needed to do a job well.

Here are some common ergonomic techniques that may help you:

- Adjust the computer display to find an angle with the least glare. Reducing glare reduces the chance of eyestrain.
- Adjust the height of the display and the copy stand, if you use one, so that you do not need to strain your back and neck as you work.
- Adjust the keyboard so that you can keep your wrists straight. If you work for a long period of time with your wrists bent, you risk inflaming your wrist tendons and making them sore.

An ergonomic environment keeps physical fatigue and eyestrain to a minimum. If you spend long periods of time at a microcomputer, consider what you can do to make your job less physically demanding. By designing a good computing environment, you can maintain a consistent quality of work and enhance your performance.

Review

1. The five hardware devices that make up a microcomputer are _____, _____, _____, _____, and _____.

2. True or False: The enhanced keyboard has fewer keys than the regular keyboard.

3. The letter K stands for _____. The letters MB stand for _____.

4. The screen on which the computer displays text is called a _____.

5. Three common types of printers are _____, _____, and _____.

6. True or False: The device that stores the greatest amount of text is called a hard disk.

7. True or False: WordPerfect 5.1 is an example of an operating system.

8. The science of keeping your work environment safe, efficient, and comfortable is _____.

9. True or False: By reducing the chance of eyestrain and making your work environment comfortable, you can enhance your keyboarding speed and accuracy and the quality of your work.

Lesson 2

Starting WordPerfect 5.1 and Printing Text

To complete each lesson in this book, you need to know how to start WordPerfect 5.1, identify the edit screen, keyboard your text, and use the save and print commands. You also need to know how to end the program.

Let's start by learning how to start WordPerfect 5.1.

Starting WordPerfect 5.1

You start WordPerfect 5.1 in one of two ways, depending upon whether or not your computer has a hard disk. The instructions in the following table show how to start WordPerfect 5.1 with and without a hard disk.

TABLE 2.1

If your computer does not have a hard disk, but has two floppy disk drives (A and B), start WordPerfect 5.1 by following these instructions:	1. Place the DOS diskette in the A drive.
	2. Switch the computer on.
	3. Keyboard the current date and press Enter.
	4. Keyboard the time and press Enter.
	   RESULT: The *A prompt* (**A>**) then appears in the top-left corner of your screen.
	5. Take the DOS diskette out of the A drive.
	6. Place the WordPerfect 5.1 Program 1 diskette in drive A.
	7. Place the data disk in drive B.
	8. Keyboard **B** and press Enter.
	   RESULT: The *B prompt* (**B>**) appears on the screen.
	9. Keyboard **A:WP** and press Enter.
	10. Follow the instructions that appear on the screen.
	   RESULT: The edit screen like the one shown in Figure 2.1 should appear. If it does not, contact your instructor or your technical support person.

If your computer system has a hard disk, start WordPerfect 5.1 by following these instructions:	1. Turn on your system.
	   RESULT: two possible messages could appear on your screen:
	   a. If a menu appears, follow its instructions for starting WordPerfect 5.1.
	   b. If the *C prompt* (**C>**) appears, keyboard **WP** and press Enter.
	   RESULT: The edit screen like the one shown in Figure 2.1 should appear. If it does not, contact your instructor or your technical support person.
	2. Place the data disk in drive B.
	   NOTE: If your microcomputer has only one drive, place the data disk in that drive.

Follow the steps in Table 2.1 that apply to your computer system, and then proceed to the next section.

What Is the Edit Screen?

The edit screen shown in Figure 2.1 is where you keyboard text. When you start WordPerfect 5.1, the edit screen is blank except for a line of information, called the *status line*, located in the lower-right corner. The small blinking dash, called the *cursor*, appears in the top-left corner.

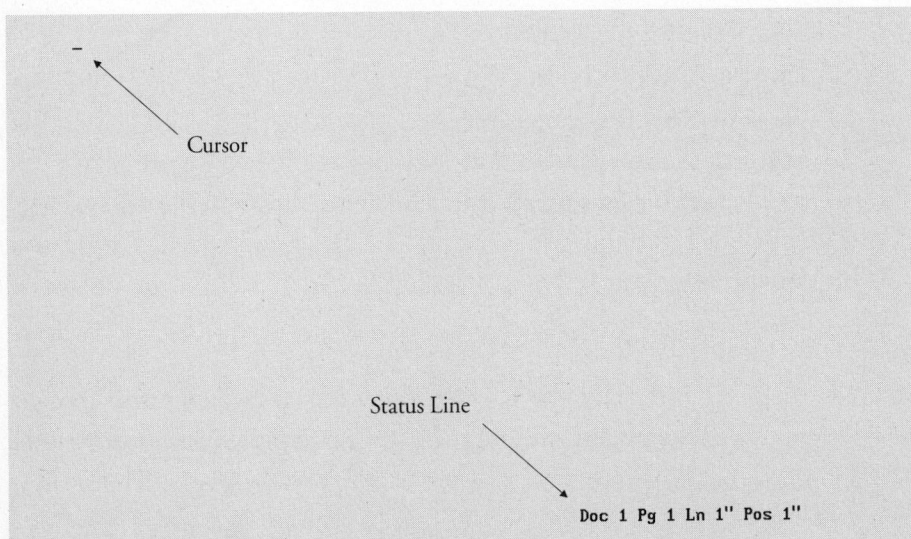

Cursor

Status Line

Doc 1 Pg 1 Ln 1" Pos 1"

FIGURE 2.1

The WordPerfect 5.1 edit screen appears when you start the program.

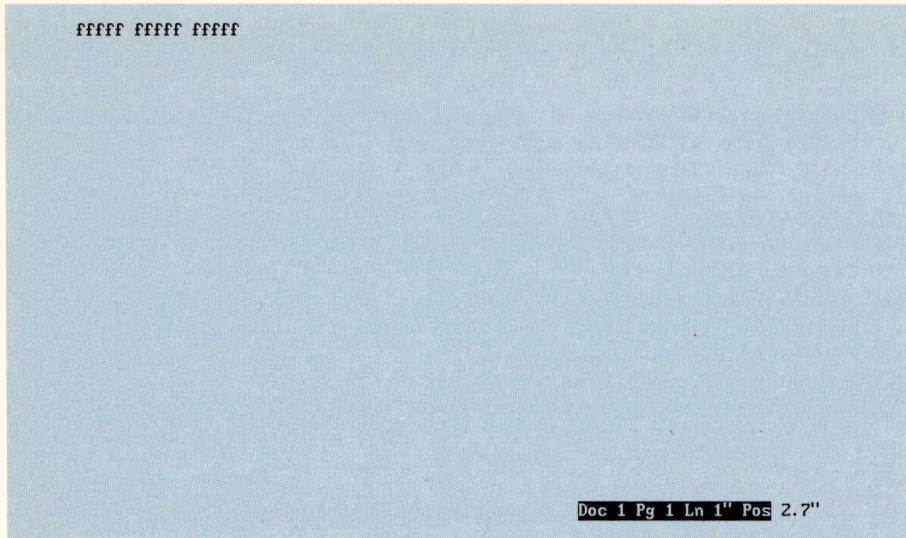

```
fffff fffff fffff
```

FIGURE 2.2
Your edit screen now contains three sets of f's on one line.

```
                                          Doc 1 Pg 1 Ln 1" Pos 2.7"
```

When you keyboard text, the text appears on the screen next to the cursor. For example, place your left index finger on the letter **f** and do the following:

Press the **f** key five times with a brief, quick touch.

RESULT: The letters **fffff** appear on the screen.

To keyboard a space, use the spacebar as shown in the next section.

Using the Spacebar

The spacebar permits you to leave space between words and letters. Use your right thumb to strike the spacebar with a sharp, quick touch. For example, place your right thumb on the spacebar and follow these steps:

1. Press the spacebar once.

   RESULT: The cursor moves one space to the right.

2. Press the **f** key five times.

3. Press the spacebar once.

4. Press the **f** key five more times.

   RESULT: Your screen will now look like the one in Figure 2.2.

   To keyboard a new line, use the Enter key as shown in the next section. (Later you will learn how WordPerfect 5.1 can automatically "wrap" text on the screen for you.)

Using the Enter Key

Enter

The Enter key is the large key labeled *Enter*, and is located just below the Backspace key (labeled ←). To use the Enter key, follow these instructions:

1. Press the Enter key.

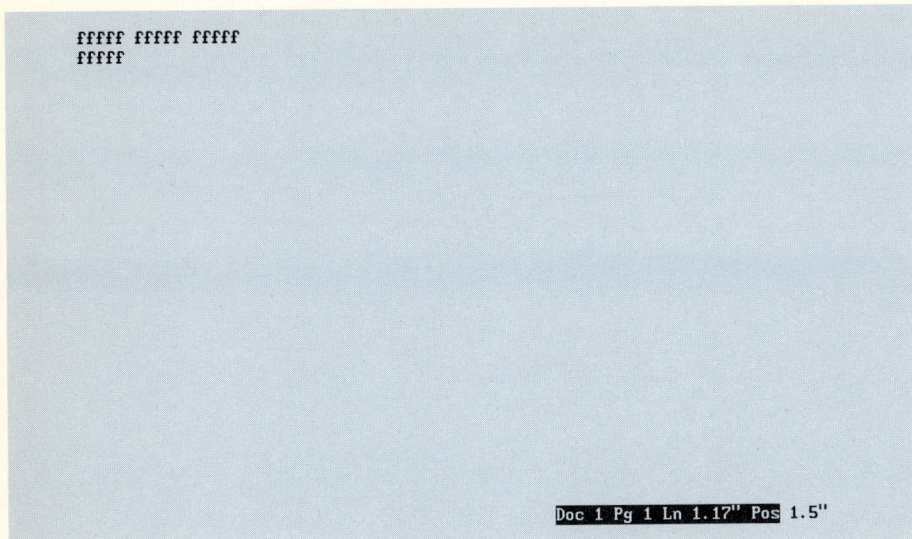

fffff fffff fffff
fffff

Doc 1 Pg 1 Ln 1.17" Pos 1.5"

FIGURE 2.3
Your edit screen now contains f's on two lines.

RESULT: The cursor moves down to the next line. You can now enter a second line of text.

2. Press the **f** key five times.

   RESULT: The screen now looks like the one in Figure 2.3.

   NOTE: The Enter key can be used to insert a blank line between rows.

   That's all there is to keyboarding text, numbers, and symbols. Before keyboarding more text, however, you need to know how to use Word-Perfect 5.1 function keys so that you can save and print what you keyboard.

Using WordPerfect 5.1 Function Keys and Menus

WordPerfect 5.1's *function keys* are those keys labeled F1, F2, F3, and so on up to F12. (Some keyboards have only 10 function keys. Having only 10 function keys does not limit your use of WordPerfect 5.1.) Function keys enable you to do many word processing tasks, such as save and print text, or end the program.

You can use functions keys in one of two ways: you either press the key alone or you press another key with it. For example, to save a document, you press one key—the Save key (F10). However, to print a document you press two keys—the Shift key and F7. Such key combinations are shown in this text with a hyphen, as in Shift-F7.

You should also be aware that instead of using function keys to operate WordPerfect 5.1, you can use a hand-held device, called a *mouse*. Most WordPerfect 5.1 users choose not to use a mouse because, they claim, it slows down their keyboarding speed. However, if you are interested in

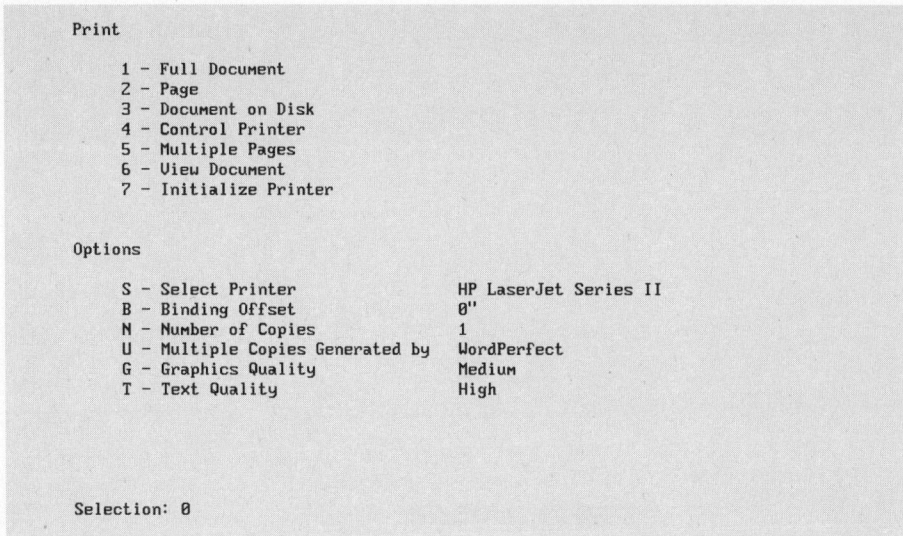

```
Print

    1 - Full Document
    2 - Page
    3 - Document on Disk
    4 - Control Printer
    5 - Multiple Pages
    6 - View Document
    7 - Initialize Printer


Options

    S - Select Printer              HP LaserJet Series II
    B - Binding Offset              0"
    N - Number of Copies            1
    U - Multiple Copies Generated by  WordPerfect
    G - Graphics Quality            Medium
    T - Text Quality                High




Selection: 0
```

FIGURE 2.4

The Print menu allows you to print your lesson.

using a mouse, refer to *Appendix A: Using Pull-Down Menus and the Mouse.*

When you use either a mouse or function keys to command Word-Perfect 5.1, the program responds with prompts or menus.

Using WordPerfect 5.1 Prompts and Menus

Each time you execute a command in WordPerfect 5.1, one of two things appears: either a prompt (at the bottom of the screen) or a menu. For example, when you press the Save key ([F10]), the following prompt appears in the bottom-left corner of the screen:

Document to be saved:

This prompt enables you to give a name to the document.

Other commands display an entire menu temporarily on the screen. For example, when you use the Print command ([Shift]-[F7]), the menu shown in Figure 2.4 appears. Your document is still available; it is just covered temporarily while you make a selection. Each option on a menu starts with a number, followed by a highlighted letter, such as **1 – F** (for 1 Full Document). Keyboarding either **1** or **F** will tell WordPerfect to print every page of your document.

In every lesson of this book, you are shown exactly what function keys to press to do a task. If you press the wrong key and a menu appears that you do not want, you simply press the Cancel key ([F1]) and WordPerfect will immediately return you to where you were before you pressed the command key.

Let's now look at the function keys you will use to save and print a document and to leave the program.

How to Save a Document

Although you can look at everything that you keyboard on the screen, the text actually exists only in your computer's memory (RAM) and will vanish if you turn off the computer. For this reason, you need to save your lessons on a floppy disk by using the Save key ($\boxed{\text{F10}}$).

Since the many different kinds of microcomputer keyboards have their special computing keys in various places, this book will not give you instructions for positioning your fingers on the function keys. You need to locate the function keys on your keyboard and strike them in a way that is comfortable for you.

To save this lesson (the two lines of f's), follow these steps:

1. Place a data disk in drive B (the right or lower drive), if it is not already there. If you have only one drive, place the disk in that drive.

2. Press the Save key ($\boxed{\text{F10}}$) in a way that is comfortable for you.
   RESULT: You should see this prompt in the lower-left corner of your screen:

   `Document to be saved:`

   NOTE: If you press the wrong function key by accident, press the Cancel key ($\boxed{\text{F1}}$) to cancel the command.

3. Keyboard the name B:LESSON2, then press $\boxed{\text{Enter}}$.
   NOTE: If you have only one drive, keyboard the name A:LESSON2. When the following message:

   `B:\LESSON2`

   appears at the bottom of the screen, the document is saved and you can print it.

How to Print a Document

To print this lesson, use the WordPerfect 5.1 Print command ($\boxed{\text{Shift}}$-$\boxed{\text{F7}}$) by following these steps:

1. Press $\boxed{\text{Shift}}$-$\boxed{\text{F7}}$. (Hold down the left $\boxed{\text{Shift}}$ key and press $\boxed{\text{F7}}$ briefly. Then release the $\boxed{\text{Shift}}$ key.)
   RESULT: The Print menu appears, as shown in Figure 2.4.
   NOTE: If you press the wrong function key by accident, press the Cancel key ($\boxed{\text{F1}}$) to cancel the command.

2. Keyboard 1 to print the document.
   If the printer does not start working, it is probably either not turned on or not correctly hooked up. Contact your instructor or technical support person. The final step in this lesson is to leave the program.

How to Exit WordPerfect 5.1

To end the program (and this lesson), follow these steps:

1. Press the Exit key ([F7]).

   RESULT: The following prompt appears in the lower-left corner of your screen:

   Save Document? Yes (No)

   NOTE: If you press the wrong function key by accident, press the Cancel key ([F1]) to cancel the command.

2. Keyboard **N**. You have already saved the document.

   RESULT: The following prompt appears in the lower-left corner of your screen:

   Exit WP? No (Yes)

3. Keyboard **Y**.

   The screen will now be blank except for a DOS command prompt in the upper-left corner. You have saved your document and exited from WordPerfect 5.1.

   Congratulations! You have just performed four of the most important word processing tasks: You have: (1) entered WordPerfect 5.1, (2) saved a document, (3) printed a document, and (4) exited the program. You will perform all of these tasks in every lesson until they become second nature.

2

Keyboarding the Alphabet with WordPerfect 5.1

Lesson 3   New Keys: a, s, d, f, j, k, l, ;

Starting WordPerfect 5.1

To start WordPerfect 5.1 and do Lesson 3, follow these two steps:

1. Start WordPerfect 5.1. (For detailed instructions on starting WordPerfect 5.1, see Lesson 2.)

2. Place your data disk in drive B, if the disk is not already there. **NOTE:** If you have only one drive, place the disk in that drive.

Home Position

The home position provides a base from which most strokes are made, enabling you to keyboard without looking at either the keyboard or the display monitor. While this is the way experts key, you cannot be expected to do so when you are learning the keyboard. It takes hundreds of practice hours before you will be able to keyboard without looking at the keys.

To place your hands in the home position, lightly place the little finger of the left hand on the **A** key and the left index finger on the **F** key. Then place the little finger of the right hand on the **;** key and the right index finger on the **J** key.

Keyboarding

With your fingers in the home position, strike each key with the appropriate finger. Be sure to press the spacebar where a space is shown. To move to the next line, strike the [Enter] key with the fourth finger of your right hand. Do not key line numbers. Key each line once.

```
1. jj jj ff ff kk kk dd dd ll ll ss ss ;; ;; aa aa jjj fff kkk;
2. aa ;; ss ll dd kk ff jj ja sa ka ad as ask asdfjkl; asdfjkl;
```

NOTE: If your lines do not end as shown above, you are not pressing the [Enter] key at the end of each line.

Press [Enter] at the end of each numbered line.

```
3. aaa ;;; sss lll ddd kkk fff jjj jal jak dad lad sad all kaka
4. a; sl dk fj dk sl a; a;a; slsl dkdk fjfj dkdk slsl a;a; fjfj

5. a ad add adds ads all as ask fall falls sad flask salad flak
6. ask all; add all; ask dad; add dad; ask all dads; as all ask

7. ask a dad; ask a lad; ask a lass; ask dad; ask lads; ask dad
8. as a dad all ask; all ask dad; dad asks all; dad asks a lass
```

Practice

At first you will need to watch the keyboard as you work. As you begin to feel more confident, try keying with your eyes on the book.

```
 9. a sad dad asks a lad; a sad lass asks a sad lad; all ask dad
10. dads fall as lads fall; lads add as dads add; dads add falls
11. all add; all ask; all fall; dads add; dads ask; all dads ask
12. dads fall; dad falls; all dads fall; ask a dad; ask all dads
13. lads add as dads add; all add as lads; all lads add; all add
14. all add fads; dads add ad fads; all dads add ads; ask a dad;
```

Skill Checks

Record your speed for each skill check by using the Performance Graph charts in Appendix D. Read the instructions before recording your results. (Don't record errors until you have completed the keyboard lessons.)

Time yourself (or have someone time you) for one minute (1') while you keyboard lines 15–16. Key at a comfortable speed. If you finish the lines before time is called, start over. Each completed line is equal to 12 words per minute (wpm). Use the scale below line 20 to determine the number of wpm you completed on a partial line. To calculate your total words per minute, add the number of words in a partial line to the number of words in the lines you completed. Repeat the one-minute (1') timed writings for lines 17–18 and 19–20.

```
15. as all ask all fall; as all fall ask dads; ask dad as a lad;
16. sad lads fall; sad dads fall; dads all fall; a sad dad falls

17. dad adds a salad; lads add a flask; all add flasks; ask all;
18. lads add as dads; a lass adds as dad adds; dads add a salad;

19. a lass asks a dad; a lad asks a dad; dads ask; lads all ask;
20. ask dad; ask all; add all; ask all; falls add; all dads fall
    +----+----+----+----+----+----+----+----+----+----+----+
      1    2    3    4    5    6    7    8    9   10   11   12
```

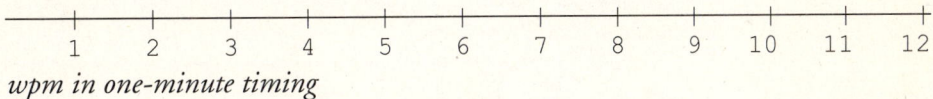

wpm in one-minute timing

Saving the Lesson

You will use the Save key ([F10]) to save a lesson.
To save the lesson, follow these steps:

1. Press the Save key ([F10]).
   NOTE: If you press the wrong function key by accident, press the Cancel key ([F1]) to cancel the command.
2. Keyboard the name B:LESSON3, then press [Enter].
   NOTE: If you have only one drive, keyboard A:LESSON3.

Printing the Lesson

You will use the Print key ([Shift]-[F7]) and 1 to print the lesson.
To print the lesson, follow these steps:

1. While holding down the [Shift] key, press [F7]. Then release the [Shift] key.
   NOTE: If you press the wrong function key by accident, press the Cancel key ([F1]) to cancel the command.
2. Keyboard 1 to print the document.

Exiting
WordPerfect 5.1

You will use the Exit key ($\boxed{\text{F7}}$) to end WordPerfect 5.1.
To end the program, follow these steps:

1. Press the Exit key ($\boxed{\text{F7}}$).
   NOTE: If you press the wrong function key by accident, press the Cancel key ($\boxed{\text{F1}}$) to cancel the command. (After this lesson, you will no longer be reminded about the Cancel key.)

2. Keyboard **N**. You have already saved the document.

3. Keyboard **Y** to leave the program.

Lesson 4

New Keys: e, c, RSK (right shift key)

Starting
WordPerfect 5.1

To start WordPerfect 5.1 and do Lesson 4, follow these two steps:

1. Start WordPerfect 5.1.

2. Place your data disk in drive B, if it is not already there.
   NOTE: If you have only one drive, place the disk in that drive.

Review

Keyboard each line once. If you need to locate a key, look at the keyboard.

If you make a mistake, immediately rekey the correction. For example, if you key **asl** when you should have keyed **ask**, immediately key **ask**—**aslask**. You are not required to correct mistakes until you move to Chapter 3. And don't worry if the cursor jumps to the next line before you press $\boxed{\text{Enter}}$. This is called *word wrap*, which you will learn more about in Lesson 8.

1. aa ;; ss ll dd kk ff jj asdfjkl; asdfjkl; a; sl dk fj dk sl;
2. a as a ask a add a all as all ask all add all ask as all add
3. all add; all ask; all fall; dads add; dads ask; all dads ask

Keyboarding   To strike **e**, reach up with the second finger of your left hand.

4. de ee de ded ded deed fee fees feed feel feels see seed seek
5. fell deal desk desks ease else jade leads see seed sell seal

6. seals seeds sales leaf lease leased leases dead assess added
7. see self sea safe less asked kale led lake sale assess leads

To strike **c**, reach down with the second finger of your left hand.

8. dc cc dc cad call calls class lack lacks call dad; call all;
9. cell cells case cases face faces scale access decade classes

10. jackals cackles cake cakes calf calk ceases ceased ceaseless
11. cask casks cad cads ace aces deck decked lacked called faced

To strike the **right shift key** (RSK) for capitalizing a letter, reach down with the little finger of your right hand.

12. Dad Al Della Cal Eda Ella Dale Ed; Cal asks Al as Ella calls
13. Dad calls Della; Cal calls Dale; Cass calls Al; Eda calls Ed

14. Ada called Alaska; Adela called Dallas; Alda faced a jackal;
15. Sal fell; Cadal led; Cass asked Edsel; Della lacked a lease;

Practice

16. Dad led all as a lad; Cal called Al as a lead; Al feels safe
17. Dale called Cal; Cal added a fee as a deal; Ed led all sales

18. Al asked a class; Ed called leads; Cal asked leads; Ed calls
19. Dad added a sales fee as a deal; Dale called Della as a lead

```
20. Dad faced a safe sea as a lad; Al feels safe as Dad led all;
21. All feel safe; all seek a sales deal; all seek Ed as a lead;

22. Ask all classes; seek sales leads; call leads; assess sales;
23. A desk scale; a class sale; a lease fee; a safe sale; a sale

24. Al sells all safes; Della leases all desks; Eda adds a case;
25. Cal adds a class; Dale lacks a class; Eda leads all classes;
```

Skill Checks

Take a one-minute timing on lines 26–27; then take a second one-minute timing on lines 28–29.

```
26. Dad led all lease sales; Cal led all else; Ella seeks leads;
27. Ella feels a jade case; Cal sells jade cases; Ed sells jade;

28. Dale sells safes; Della leases desks; Eda seals desk scales;
29. Ella added a desk scale as a sales deal; call Cal; ask Dale;
```

```
    +    +    +    +    +    +    +    +    +    +    +    +
    1    2    3    4    5    6    7    8    9    10   11   12
```

wpm in one-minute timing

Saving the Lesson

To save the lesson, follow these steps:

1. Press the Save key (F10).
2. Keyboard the name B:LESSON4, then press Enter.
   NOTE: If you have only one drive, keyboard A:LESSON4.

Printing the Lesson

To print the lesson, follow these steps:

1. While holding down the Shift key, press F7. Then release the Shift key.
2. Keyboard 1 to print the document.

Exiting WordPerfect 5.1

To end the program, follow these steps:

1. Press the Exit key (F7).
2. Keyboard N. You have already saved the document.
3. Keyboard Y to leave the program.

Lesson 5   New Keys: o, . (period), LSK (left shift key)

Starting WordPerfect 5.1

1. Start WordPerfect 5.1.
2. Place your data disk in drive B, if it is not already there.

Review

```
1. faced access called classes self seeds seal leaf leads lakes
2. added asked call case class fee feel less sale sales see ask
3. ask all dads; add fall classes; see a jade sea seal; ask Dee
```

Keyboarding

To strike **o**, reach up with the third finger of your right hand.

```
4. lo oo lo look loss also local of off also do does sold so do
5. close closed load losses coffee coal coded cold cook look of

6. flood loaded loads looked looks folks foods oak odd sole old
7. cool food loose code lose sock look also do of so does local
```

To strike . (period), reach down with the third finger of your right hand.

To end a sentence correctly, space twice after the period. Do not space before the period.

8. Ed cooked. Della looked sad. Dad closed cases. Al called.
9. Dale looked old. Ella sold food. Dad loaded old oak desks.

To strike the **left shift key** (LSK) for capitalizing a letter, reach down with the little finger of your left hand.

10. Dad looked cold. Della cooked food. Ella sold cold coffee.
11. Eels look so cold. Jackals look so old. Ed also sold jade.

12. Lee loaded. Les looked. Jack fell. Jess asked. Jack led.
13. Jack sold desks. Jeff also sold coal. Les also sells seed.

14. Les closed all local lakes. Lee led Jack. Les sold a sock.
15. Jack sold coffee. Jake loaded old desks. Jess cooked food.

Practice

As soon as possible, try to key these sentences without watching the keyboard.

16. Jess looked odd. Lee closed all food cases. Al feels cold.
17. Les also called all old local folks. All loaded local coal.

18. Jess looked so sad. Folks loaded cold food. All look cold.
19. Jeff sold old coffee cases. Ed sold desks. Al sells seeds.

20. Sal sold old seeds. Sal also sold lead. Sal also sold ads.
21. Al also sold food. All feel so cold. Les closed all lakes.

22. All local lakes look flooded. All coffee cases look so old.
23. Lee sold clocks. Jeff closed deals. Ed closed sales deals.

24. Ed sold old local jade clocks. Ed closed local sales deals.
25. Local folks looked sad as Della loaded all old coffee cases.

Skill Checks

Take a one-minute timing on lines 26–28. Key at a comfortable rate—neither too slow nor too fast.

26. Della sold cocoa; Dale cooked cod; Ella coded old oak cases.
27. Jack also looked sad as folks assessed dead sea seal losses.
28. Jess closed all loose old oases. Al sold a local coffee ad.

```
  +    +    +    +    +    +    +    +    +    +    +    +
  1    2    3    4    5    6    7    8    9   10   11   12
```
wpm in one-minute timing

Saving the Lesson

To save the lesson, follow these steps:

1. Press the Save key ([F10]).
2. Keyboard the name B:LESSON5, then press [Enter].

Printing the Lesson

To print the lesson, follow these steps:

1. While holding down the [Shift] key, press [F7]. Then release the [Shift] key.
2. Keyboard **1** to print the document.

*Exiting
WordPerfect 5.1*

To end the program, follow these steps:

1. Press the Exit key ([F7]).
2. Keyboard **N**. You have already saved the document.
3. Keyboard **Y** to leave the program.

Lesson 6

New Keys: t, g, and b

*Starting
WordPerfect 5.1*

1. Start WordPerfect 5.1.
2. Place your data disk in drive B, if it is not already there.

Review

1. Ed sells oak; Lee sells cola; Adel sold ads; Cass sold food;
2. Al cooked cold food. Ed looked cold. Cal sold cold coffee.
3. Ed looked sad as Al sold old oak cases. Jack looked so old.

Keyboarding   To strike **t**, reach up with the first finger of your left hand.

4. ft tt ft to too told took tool test tell task tall talk take
5. coat cost foot last late left lost lots salt sets state etc.

6. at flat felt feet fast fact east date data cast acts act let
7. dated effect jet latest lot sat set staff states stool total

To strike **g**, reach to the right with the first finger of your left hand.

8. fg gg fg gas gasses glass go goes dog dogs leg legs age ages
9. gold golf good goal goals glad edge legal lodge logs college

10. egg eggs logo gee ago ego colleges catalog log edges glasses
11. get gets got aged stage gag gadget gases gasket gate cottage

To strike **b**, reach down with the first finger of your left hand.

Remember to space once after a semicolon (;) and twice after a period.

12. fb bb fb be bed based baseball base ball bad backs back able
13. beds beef bell black label labels lb. lbs. block blocks book

14. bag bags beat belt ballet ballot battle backed stable tables
15. job jobs object objects books booklet booklets boat Bob debt

Practice

16. Dad sold all bottles; Ed collected a fee; Al settled a debt.
17. Take a state test; be set to act; be good to a lot of folks.

18. Collect old objects; select good catalogs; locate all books.
19. Take a look at a catalog; select good colleges; take a seat.

20. Dad got a golf bag. Bob got a boat. Al collects baseballs.
21. Bob asked Kate. Joe also asked Kate. Todd also dated Ella.

22. Kate got a college sales job. Jake sold old football books.
23. Jess selected a good baseball booklet. Kate located a coat.

24. Dad took old bottles. Lee talked to Ella. Ed located data.
25. Jeff located a fast food sales job. Jeff sells beef steaks.

26. Bess got a good job at a college. Ed asked to be back late.
27. Ed took a test to be selected to go to a good state college.

28. Joe selected a black steel table. Dad got a gold golf ball.
29. All states stock job test booklets. Ed got good legal data.

Skill Checks

Take a one-minute timing on lines 30–31; then take a second one-minute timing on lines 32–33. To do your best in these timings, key at a comfortable speed.

30. Dee collects glass objects. Sal collects football catalogs.
31. Dad left a lake estate to Kate. Dale located a cottage lot.

32. Age affects all old objects. Kate collected old oak tables.
33. Jess located a good state lodge. Cal selected a black coat.

| 1 | 2 | 3 | 4 | 5 | 6 | 7 | 8 | 9 | 10 | 11 | 12 |

wpm in one-minute timing

Saving the Lesson

To save the lesson, follow these steps:

1. Press the Save key ([F10]).
2. Keyboard the name B:LESSON6, then press [Enter].

Printing the Lesson

To print the lesson, follow these steps:

1. While holding down the [Shift] key, press [F7]. Then release the [Shift] key.
2. Keyboard 1 to print the document.

Exiting
WordPerfect 5.1

To end the program, follow these steps:

1. Press the Exit key ([F7]).
2. Keyboard **N**. You have already saved the document.
3. Keyboard **Y** to leave the program.

Lesson 7   New Keys: i, u, m, and , (comma)

Starting
WordPerfect 5.1

1. Start WordPerfect 5.1.
2. Place your data disk in drive B, if it is not already there.

Review

1. Kate got a set of job booklets. Ed located a state college.
2. Jack took a test to get a job. Della took a job at a lodge.
3. Jed collected facts; Les located stocks; Della tested tools;

K e y b o a r d i n g   To strike i, reach up with the second finger of your right hand.

4. ki ii ki if is it its ill ice idea ideas aid bid bit fit kid
5. I bill sit skill till did like life list little office ideal

6. Jill assist big details files side title bids lie cities kit
7. basis field still facilities file fill listed oil said basic

To strike **u**, reach up with the first finger of your right hand.

---

8. ju uu ju just full due but out us use used because suggested
9. uses usual soul luck judge auto audit guest duties tube fuel

---

Try to complete each sentence without watching the keyboard.

---

10. budget club cut actual successful success suggest subject us
11. Sue got a good club steak. Al suggested a big side of beef.

To strike **m**, reach down with the first finger of your right hand.

---

12. jm mm jm am made make me same most come models almost become
13. makes model small meet meets seems memo most team bottom met

14. accommodate mass meal damage game came stem image item times
15. Mail a small model kit to James. Mail me a football ticket.

To strike **,** (comma), reach down with the second finger of your right hand. Space once after, not before, the comma.

---

16. k,k k,k Kodiak, Alaska, seems so old. But, I still like it.
17. small automobiles, domestic films, famous guests, good ideas
18. blue suit, musical title, small office, cold milk, take aim,
19. I collected kits, games, gifts, etc. I built custom models.

Practice

---

20. Fido, a small dog, seems ill. Jet, a black cat, got a cold.
21. Julie Adams suggested a good idea. It could also be useful.

22. Jack discussed it also. Sue said to assume a good attitude.
23. Ed Lee suggested a list of budget items. Bob missed a meal.

24. Bill submitted a detailed list. I deducted all team claims.
25. It takes time to build a successful team. I made a mistake.

```
26.  I filed medical bills.   Ted calculated all justified claims.
27.  I assumed all office sites must be sold.   Al issued details.
```

Skill Checks

Take a one-minute timing on lines 28–30.

```
28.  Jim asked Miss Lisa Gabel, a statistical aide, to assist us.
29.  Gail cooked a beautiful club steak; Jack made a small salad.
30.  Ted sold a beautiful custom auto to a model automobile club.
```

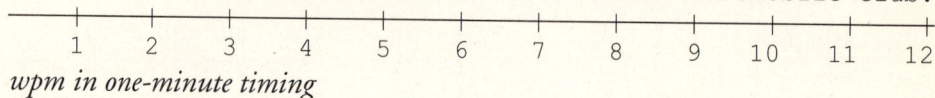

```
    +    +    +    +    +    +    +    +    +    +    +    +
    1    2    3    4    5    6    7    8    9   10   11   12
```

wpm in one-minute timing

Saving the Lesson

To save the lesson, follow these steps:

1. Press the Save key ([F10]).
2. Keyboard the name B:LESSON7, then press [Enter].

Printing the Lesson

To print the lesson, follow these steps:

1. While holding down the [Shift] key, press [F7]. Then release the [Shift] key.
2. Keyboard 1 to print the document.

Exiting WordPerfect 5.1

To end the program, follow these steps:

1. Press the Exit key ([F7]).
2. Keyboard N. You have already saved the document.
3. Keyboard Y to leave the program.

3

Keyboarding the Alphabet and Moving the Cursor

Lesson 8   Moving the Cursor and Making Corrections with WordPerfect 5.1

When you are keyboarding text, you will sometimes want to move the cursor around on the screen without affecting the text you have keyboarded. As shown in Figure 8.1, the *cursor movement keys* are the arrow keys (⬆, ⬇, ➡, and ⬅) on the keyboard. Pressing one of these keys moves the cursor one position in the direction of the arrow.

For example, follow these steps:

1. Keyboard these two lines:

   ```
   Julie Adams suggested a good idea.
   It takes time to build a successful team.
   ```

2. Press the up arrow (⬆) once.
   RESULT: The cursor moves up to the first line.
   NOTE: If the number **8** appears instead, you need to press the NumLock key once to turn NumLock off. Then repeat step 2.

3. Press the left arrow (⬅) until the cursor is on the **A** of **Adams**.

4. Press the right arrow key (➡) and the down arrow key (⬇) until the cursor is positioned just after the period of the second sentence.
   As you practice moving the cursor, you will become more familiar with this feature of WordPerfect 5.1.

FIGURE 8.1 *Enhanced keyboards have two Delete keys and two sets of cursor movement keys.*

Using Word Wrap

Whenever you reach the end of a line, WordPerfect 5.1 automatically moves the cursor to the next line. This automatic return feature is known as *word wrap*. By using word wrap, the only time you will need to press the Enter key is when you want to start a new paragraph or keyboard a short line.

For example, keyboard the following paragraph without pressing the Enter key at the end of a line:

```
Julie Adams suggested a good idea.  It takes time
to build a successful team.  Julie Adams suggested
a good idea.  It takes time to build a successful
team.
```

NOTE: Line endings may vary.

Did you notice that when the cursor reached the right margin it automatically jumped to the next line? You will get plenty of practice using word wrap in the coming lessons.

Correcting Mistakes As You Keyboard

As you keyboard text, you may at times "feel" that you have made a mistake. When this happens, you can immediately correct your mistake by using either the backspace key or the delete key. Let's look at these keys more closely.

Using the Backspace and Delete keys
Backspace Del

Backspace. The Backspace key is usually above the Enter key. This key deletes any character to the immediate left of the cursor and moves all following characters to the left by one position.

Delete. A regular keyboard has one Del key, but the enhanced keyboard has two, as shown in Figure 8.1.

The ⌐Del⌐ key deletes any character above the cursor. If you continue to hold down the ⌐Del⌐ key, it will *delete* the text to the right of the cursor one character at a time. Because the ⌐Del⌐ key deletes text above the cursor, you need to first move the cursor with the cursor movement keys (⌐↑⌐, ⌐↓⌐, ⌐→⌐, ⌐←⌐) before you can delete the mistake.

For example, try the following exercise:

1. On a new line, keyboard this text:

   `Bill sud`

2. Press the ⌐Backspace⌐ key once.
   RESULT: The **d** in **sud** is erased.

3. Keyboard the following:

   `bmitted a detailed mist.`

   RESULT: The word **submitted** is correctly keyboarded.
   You now note that the word **mist** should be the word **list**.

4. Press the ⌐←⌐ until the cursor is on the **m** in **mist**.

5. Press the ⌐Del⌐ key.
   The **m** is erased and the word moves to the left one space.
   NOTE: If you press the ⌐Del⌐ key, and a period (.) appears before the **m**, you need to press the ⌐NumLock⌐ key once to turn off ⌐NumLock⌐. Then press ⌐←⌐ once to move the cursor to the period (.), and press the ⌐Del⌐ key twice to delete the period and the **m**.

6. Keyboard the letter **l**.
   RESULT: WordPerfect 5.1 inserts the **l**. Your sentence should now look like this:

   `Bill submitted a detailed list.`

If after keyboarding text you immediately realize that you have made a mistake, correct it by using the ⌐Backspace⌐ or ⌐Del⌐—whichever is more convenient for you.

Review

1. To move the cursor to the right, press _____.
2. To move the cursor to the left, press _____.
3. To move the cursor up, press _____.
4. To move the cursor down, press _____.
5. True or False: To move the cursor to the next line, you *always* have to press the ⌐Enter⌐ key. Explain your answer.

6. Multiple choice: The ⎡Backspace⎤ key erases the character (a) above the cursor (b) to the left of the cursor.

7. To erase a character that you have just entered, you decide to use the ⎡Del⎤ key. What key do you have to press first? Explain your answer.

Lesson 9   New Keys: h, n, and y

Starting WordPerfect 5.1

1. Start WordPerfect 5.1.
2. Place your data disk in drive B, if it is not already there.

Review

1. Bill asked me to get a cold glass of milk. It satisfies me.
2. A local official issued a detailed message to both colleges.
3. A judge decided Bob Bass must be at fault; Dee felt so, too.

Keyboarding

To strike h, reach to the left with the first finger of your right hand.

4. jh hh jh he had has his high him held health head home homes
5. should such check hesitate hold schools checks sheets height

6. she the ahead much those that them these this touch although
7. attached bath beach behalf bushels catch chest child highest

To strike **n**, reach down with the first finger of your right hand.

```
 8.  jn nn jn no not needs net on and been can in on one into inn
 9.  men maintenance beginning connection find being need selling

10.  attention gentlemen enclosing annual cannot national man end
11.  name nice night none noon note often using until union taken
```

To strike **y**, reach up with the first finger of your right hand.

```
12.  jy yy jy yet you may day days say buy system actually by Amy
13.  my they today study delay easy fully actually eyes yes loyal

14.  immediately family any many only city fly daily money likely
15.  yield usually tiny totally maybe okay sky style successfully
```

Practice

```
16.  Andy Jung is seeking a job to finance his college education.
17.  One day Kaye met a client at a national management luncheon.

18.  The gentleman, Ty Lee, indicated that he needed a hotel key.
19.  In addition to money, the job included educational benefits.

20.  Sally decided to take the job.  I contacted the same agency.
21.  Angela and my cousin, Anita Lee, decided to go to the dance.

22.  They met Deana and Daniel at a society dance and had a ball.
23.  All my students can attend the alumni association luncheons.

24.  My accounting assignment is due.  He must submit a solution.
25.  Gene needs a license to fly, fish, hunt, and sell sailboats.

26.  Stacey signed a check.  Joyce may not cash it until Tuesday.
27.  You should insist on a settlement on behalf of each student.
```

Whenever you realize you have made an error, be sure to correct the error immediately.

```
28.  The National Health Institute is holding its annual meeting.
29.  Sally should take one day at a time.  Anne, Amy, and Ty did.

30.  Selling to ad agencies is a challenge.  Gayle sold many ads.
31.  Ed got a beautiful tan.  Jack and I fished.  Ty tended sail.
```

Skill Checks

```
32.  Betty Young is my best teaching aide; she can do a good job.
33.  Jane set sail, at last, in a still sea.  She landed at dusk.
34.  Floyd sailed and landed on an island.  He and Jill got lost.
```
```
      1    2    3    4    5    6    7    8    9   10   11   12
```
wpm in one-minute timing

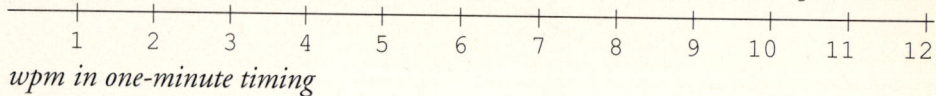

Cursor Movement Practice

Follow these steps:

1. Move the cursor to the letter **Y** in the name **Young** in line 32.
2. Move the cursor to the **A** in **Anne** in line 29.
3. Move the cursor to the end of the lesson.

Saving the Lesson

To save the lesson, follow these steps:

1. Press the Save key ([F10]).
2. Keyboard the name B:LESSON9, then press [Enter].

Printing the Lesson

To print the lesson, follow these steps:

1. While holding down the [Shift] key, press [F7]. Then release the [Shift] key.
2. Keyboard **1** to print the document.

Exiting WordPerfect 5.1

To end the program, follow these steps:

1. Press the Exit key ([F7]).
2. Keyboard **N**. You have already saved the document.
3. Keyboard **Y** to leave the program.

Lesson 10   New Keys: r and v

Starting WordPerfect 5.1

1. Start WordPerfect 5.1.
2. Place your data disk in drive B, if it is not already there.

Review

```
1. Jim and Linda sold cotton candy; Amy and Dale sold iced tea.
2. One finds a college education is not an end but a beginning.
3. Yes, I did see them go last night.  Most of them took tents.
```

K e y b o a r d i n g

To strike **r**, reach up with the first finger of your left hand.

```
4. fr rr fr for from Mr. or our their there area first form her
5. more order other year your yours after course before further

6. dear letter sincerely truly during return rate records rates
7. yourself yard urge urban uniform truth turn under understand
```

To strike **v**, reach down with the first finger of your left hand.

```
8.  fv vv fv van valley valve valuable various vote visit volume
9.  have above give advise believe division given receive Steven
10. available convenience even invoice having save involves very
11. vast vice vital visual visitors voltage voluntary vocational
```

Practice

By now you should be looking at the keyboard less frequently.

12. Early every morning my dog and I run to the market and back.
13. On a clear morning you can see the sun rise over the garden.

14. Brent ordered a breakfast of orange juice, bacon, and toast.
15. Al asked for a large order of ham and eggs. Ed cooked them.

16. This year Henry made arrangements for a training conference.
17. My staff advised me to be sure that I received meal tickets.

18. Reservations for this year are closed. I must change yours.
19. One of our freedoms is the right to elect our state senator.

20. I am sending Al my best stereo records to take to the dance.
21. It is my recommendation that you attend a vocational school.

22. I obtained a brochure. It outlined all engineering courses.
23. Your secretary, Amy Baker, is a valuable asset to our staff.

24. I have information that your materials are to arrive by air.
25. Your order has been delayed by a recent industrial accident.

26. Every day Helen, my family, and I jog to the river and back.
27. Mrs. Charles, there are several reasons to charge you a fee.

28. The summer is a fine time for boating, sailing, and surfing.
29. Ed listed several advantages to joining the Science Society.

Skill Checks

30. My conversation at the office resulted in a dealer contract.
31. Ben, Fred, Jack, and Glen sailed our boat to a distant lake.
32. Dr. Steven Hiscott made reservations at the convention rate.

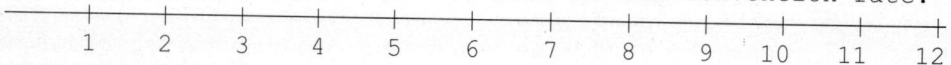

```
+----+----+----+----+----+----+----+----+----+----+----+----+
  1    2    3    4    5    6    7    8    9   10   11   12
```
wpm in one-minute timing

Word Wrap Practice   Use word wrap. Your line endings may vary.

There are several advantages to obtaining a brochure before you make a reservation. The first is that it informs you about events. The second is that it is free.

Saving the Lesson

To save the lesson, follow these steps:

1. Press the Save key ([F10]).
2. Keyboard the name B:LESSON10, then press [Enter].

Printing the Lesson

To print the lesson, follow these steps:

1. While holding down the [Shift] key, press [F7]. Then release the [Shift] key.
2. Keyboard **1** to print the document.

Exiting WordPerfect 5.1

To end the program, follow these steps:

1. Press the Exit key ([F7]).
2. Keyboard **N**. You have already saved the document.
3. Keyboard **Y** to leave the program.

Lesson 11 New Keys: p and ?

Starting WordPerfect 5.1

1. Start WordPerfect 5.1.
2. Place your data disk in drive B, if it is not already there.

Review

1. Lee and Val do a good job as baby sitters; Lee is available.
2. In the future our manager, Mr. Karl, must order through you.
3. Steven can get a reduced rate by flying on a charter flight.

Keyboarding   To strike **p**, reach up with the little finger of your right hand.

4. ;p pp ;p part people per plain policy possible present price
5. company copy please program up keep past pay percent special

6. hope person product proper purpose plus post public property
7. upon typing type trip top tape support supply stop step spot

To strike **?**, use the left shift key (LSK) and reach down with the little finger of your right hand.

8. ;? ?? ;? Is it Tim? Does Mary say so? Did she? Can Ty go?
9. Is the Tournament on tonight? Can I stay to see it? Can I?

10. Are you available? Should I advise him? Is it Miss or Ms.?
11. Can I order the subscription? Does he need to see a doctor?

Practice

12. Do you think I should accept? Did he appreciate the report?
13. Did the program please you? Did Pat go up to the lake site?

14. Did Patrick go to the county fair? Did Jane? Did Jennifer?
15. Is it true that he and I are no longer friends? I hope not.

16. Did Phil say so? Can Page go? Please accept our apologies.
17. Is Frosty your dog? Does she belong to your neighbor, Paul?

18. Did the forecaster say it might rain today? Must he cancel?
19. Is the golf tournament on TV tonight? Did Dick and Lisa go?

20. Every person in my department is responsible for production.
21. I hope Stacey has an opportunity to introduce the president.

22. The cost of group hospital insurance protection is too high.
23. I appreciate your interest in my progress as a club sponsor.

24. Please type these license applications for Pat, Sue, and me.
25. I have an important telephone message for Jan. Is she home?

26. Can you picture Kelly as a professional sports photographer?
27. Does practice make perfect in all fields? Does Sally agree?

28. Computer programming is an appropriate career choice for me.
29. I hope you can help George plan for our annual office party.

Skill Checks

30. This is the most technologically advanced car on the market.
31. It offers you a special combination of efficiency and value.
32. Try my best standard sedan. Enjoy a test drive in one soon.

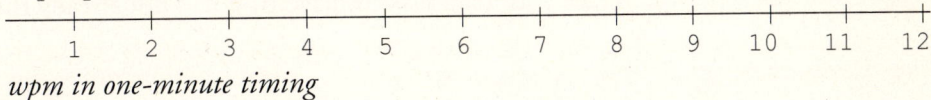

```
  +---+---+---+---+---+---+---+---+---+---+---+
  1   2   3   4   5   6   7   8   9  10  11  12
```

wpm in one-minute timing

Saving the Lesson

To save the lesson, follow these steps:

1. Press the Save key (F10).
2. Keyboard the name B:LESSON11, then press Enter.

Printing the Lesson

To print the lesson, follow these steps:

1. While holding down the Shift key, press F7. Then release the Shift key.
2. Keyboard 1 to print the document.

Exiting WordPerfect 5.1

To end the program, follow these steps:

1. Press the Exit key (F7).
2. Keyboard N. You have already saved the document.
3. Keyboard Y to leave the program.

Lesson 12   New Keys: w and x

Starting WordPerfect 5.1

1. Start WordPerfect 5.1.
2. Place your data disk in drive B, if it is not already there.

Review

1. Kevin is very tall; his sister, Becky, is on the short side.
2. Each artist is selling a sample of the latest in modern art.
3. Does the computer print an income statement for Jane to see?

Keyboarding   To strike **w**, reach up with the third finger of your left hand.

4. sw ww sw was we were when which who why will with work would
5. want well what wish week where while within without news way

6. know new now two following how however few own between shown
7. flow snow saw town won words wrote writing woman view yellow

To strike **x**, reach down with the third finger of your left hand.

8. sx xx sx tax taxes extra extend express existing except next
9. exact examination expect executive anxious boxes complex fix

10. maximum approximately expenses example expense excellent box
11. deluxe excess mix mixed index inexpensive express experience

Practice

12. Now is the time for Alex to plan a vacation in West Germany.
13. Max received a warm welcome traveling throughout Washington.

14. Is it true experience is the best teacher? Should we agree?
15. The two women were without electrical power for a whole day.

16. Workers were waiting along the highway to fix the cut wires.
17. Roxanne, Trixie, and Alexis wanted to watch the six workers.

18. I explained that we were without raincoats. She still went.
19. Dexter bought an expensive mower. Felix got a deluxe watch.

20. A good beginning sentence is important when writing a story.
21. An introductory sentence may tell you where, what, and when.

22. Max used a yellow notebook to record the weekly experiments.
23. A week of rain ruined the outdoor water show we had planned.

24. The view from the air balloon was excellent. I expected it.
25. We expected to find the extra fixture at the hardware store.

26. The severe winters caused extreme hardships on the wildlife.
27. Were you aware that some travel expenses are tax deductible?

28. My tax accountant suggested that we expand our old workshop.
29. All were anxious to get the results of the tax examinations.

Skill Checks

30. You can expect an expert in law to interview Herb carefully.
31. The warm yellow sun extended across the beautiful blue lake.
32. I got to the gate too late to see Jim land in the jumbo jet.

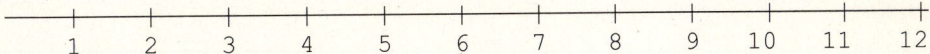

```
  +    +    +    +    +    +    +    +    +    +    +    +
  1    2    3    4    5    6    7    8    9    10   11   12
```
wpm in one-minute timing

Saving the Lesson

To save the lesson, follow these steps:

1. Press the Save key (F10).
2. Keyboard the name B:LESSON12, then press Enter .

Printing the Lesson   To print the lesson, follow these steps:

1. While holding down the ⌷Shift⌷ key, press ⌷F7⌷. Then release the ⌷Shift⌷ key.
2. Keyboard **1** to print the document.

*Exiting
WordPerfect 5.1*   To end the program, follow these steps:

1. Press the Exit key (⌷F7⌷).
2. Keyboard **N**. You have already saved the document.
3. Keyboard **Y** to leave the program.

Lesson 13   New Keys: q and z

*Starting
WordPerfect 5.1*

1. Start WordPerfect 5.1.
2. Place your data disk in drive B, if it is not already there.

Review

1. Max bought bread, wine, and cheese; and Frank bought apples.
2. Today is the age of the personal computer. It is ready now.
3. Did Janice ask if the computer store had several new models?

Keyboarding   To strike **q**, reach up with the little finger of your left hand.

4. aq qq aq quite quantity quick quiet quota quote quit quality
5. request equipment questions requested required questionnaire

6. inquiry require requesting quantity requests requisition qua
7. qualify acquired adequate banquet delinquent quarter squared

To strike **z**, reach down with the little finger of your left hand.

8. az zz az size jazz organization amazing frozen organizations
9. analyze authorization citizen dozen itemized hospitalization

10. magazine oz. prizes realize recognize sizes utilize utilized
11. prize emphasize organized realized specialized stabilization

Practice   When you are able to strike each key with the correct fingers without looking at the keyboard, you have learned to "touch" key. Here are some tips to help you develop this skill:
- Keyboard at a faster speed.
- Mentally spell each word as you keyboard it.
- Look at the keyboard only when you have to.

12. Angie analyzed the dozen new articles for the jazz magazine.
13. I did not know what questions to ask. I picked an easy one.

14. What are your requirements for organizing a summer workshop?
15. Each organization should have a copy of all award inquiries.

16. There will be many prizes awarded. Most executives qualify.
17. Do I need authorization to require a text for our tax class?

18. No, but you will need one for a new textbook in typewriting.
19. We had an inquiry today from a customer for a size ten shoe.

20. Today, many women are seeking careers as public accountants.
21. I just received a call from a company requesting quotations.

22. Anita apologized for the delinquent tax payment on her home.
23. Stacey utilized a technique requiring an inexpensive liquid.

```
24. It was quite a performance to see.  Most of us were pleased.
25. An experienced stage crew knew exactly the equipment to use.

26. Paul ordered a twelve oz. steak with baked potato and salad.
27. Beth should organize a trip to Europe before winter arrives.

28. Lucy needs to learn the language.  I suggest that she study.
29. Perhaps Suzy can borrow a film on places to visit in Europe.
```

Skill Checks

```
30. Steven, Linda, and Stacey qualified as winners at the party.
31. Terry and Angela requested that the orchestra play a number.
32. Suzanne packed the square boxes with five dozen liquid jugs.
```

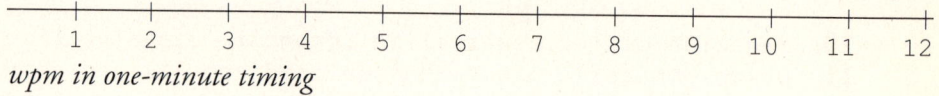

```
   1    2    3    4    5    6    7    8    9   10   11   12
```

wpm in one-minute timing

Saving the Lesson

To save the lesson, follow these steps:

1. Press the Save key (F10).
2. Keyboard the name B:LESSON13, then press Enter.

Printing the Lesson

To print the lesson, follow these steps:

1. While holding down the Shift key, press F7. Then release the Shift key.
2. Keyboard 1 to print the document.

Exiting WordPerfect 5.1

To end the program, follow these steps:

1. Press the Exit key (F7).
2. Keyboard N. You have already saved the document.
3. Keyboard Y to leave the program.

CHAPTER

4

Using WordPerfect 5.1 Function Keys

Lesson 14   Using WordPerfect 5.1 Function Keys

WordPerfect 5.1's *function keys* are the heart of WordPerfect 5.1. They enable you to carry out over 40 different word processing commands, such as Center, Bold, or Underlining.

Some WordPerfect 5.1 commands require just one keystroke; for example, the Underlining command requires pressing `F8`. Others, such as the Center command, require pressing two keys. To perform the Center command, you would press `Shift`-`F6`.

WordPerfect 5.1 has three kinds of commands: prompt, menu, and toggle commands.

Using WordPerfect 5.1 Prompt and Menu Commands

You have already worked with prompt and menu commands. For example, when you press the Save key (`F10`), the following prompt appears on the screen:

Document to be saved:

The Print menu is an example of a menu command. As you have seen, it temporarily appears on the display monitor when you press `Shift`-`F7`.

A toggle command is slightly different.

Using WordPerfect 5.1 Toggle Commands

You work a *toggle command* by pressing a function key once to turn it on and pressing it again to turn it off. Underlining (F8), Bold (F6), and CapsLock are all toggle commands. For example, to bold a word takes three steps:

1. Press the Bold key (F6) to turn it on.

2. Keyboard the word.

3. Press the Bold key to turn it off.

Unlike the alphabet, number, and symbol keys, there is no one best way to strike WordPerfect 5.1 commands—there are too many different kinds of computer keyboards. We suggest that you strike function keys in ways that are comfortable for you. Also, feel free to look at the keyboard.

You will practice many WordPerfect 5.1 toggle commands in this book to indent, bold, capitalize, and underline text. In addition, you will use menu commands to change your line spacing and tabs. Because changing tabs and line spacing is more complex than performing simple toggle commands, let's look at these tasks more closely.

Setting WordPerfect 5.1 Tabs

WordPerfect 5.1 automatically places a tab every half-inch (five spaces). You can change tabs by following these steps:

1. Press Shift - F8.

   RESULT: The Format menu appears, as shown in Figure 14.1. This menu enables you to change the format of lines, pages, or the entire document.

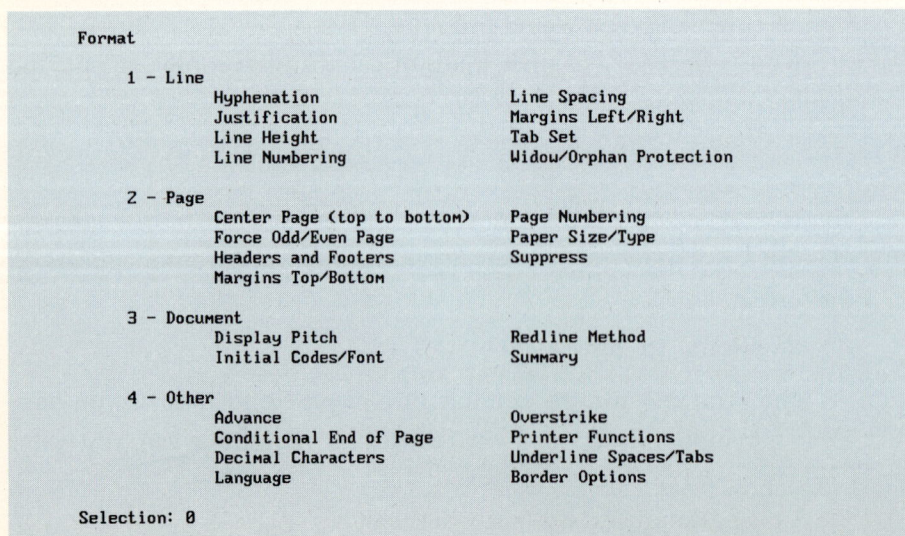

```
Format

    1 - Line
            Hyphenation                 Line Spacing
            Justification               Margins Left/Right
            Line Height                 Tab Set
            Line Numbering              Widow/Orphan Protection

    2 - Page
            Center Page (top to bottom)  Page Numbering
            Force Odd/Even Page          Paper Size/Type
            Headers and Footers          Suppress
            Margins Top/Bottom

    3 - Document
            Display Pitch                Redline Method
            Initial Codes/Font           Summary

    4 - Other
            Advance                      Overstrike
            Conditional End of Page      Printer Functions
            Decimal Characters           Underline Spaces/Tabs
            Language                     Border Options

    Selection: 0
```

FIGURE 14.1

The WordPerfect 5.1 Format menu lets you change the appearance of your document.

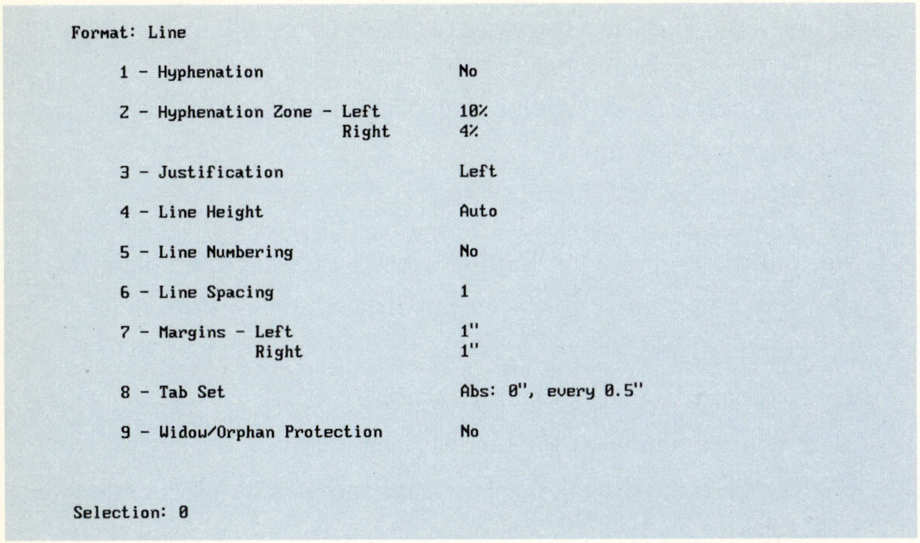

```
Format: Line

    1 - Hyphenation                    No

    2 - Hyphenation Zone - Left        10%
                         Right         4%

    3 - Justification                  Left

    4 - Line Height                    Auto

    5 - Line Numbering                 No

    6 - Line Spacing                   1

    7 - Margins - Left                 1"
                  Right                1"

    8 - Tab Set                        Abs: 0", every 0.5"

    9 - Widow/Orphan Protection        No


Selection: 0
```

FIGURE 14.2

The WordPerfect 5.1 Line Format menu lets you set tabs and line spacing.

2. Keyboard **1** to select the Line option.

RESULT: The Line Format menu appears, as shown in Figure 14.2. Among other items, this menu allows you to change line spacing, margins, and tabs.

3. Keyboard **8** to select the Tab option.

RESULT: The tab ruler appears at the bottom of the screen, as shown in Figure 14.3.

The tab ruler marks each tab by placing an **L** every half-inch (five spaces). To *set a new tab*, move the cursor to the position on the ruler where you want the tab, and keyboard **L**. (Move the cursor by pressing →.) To *delete a tab*, move the cursor to the tab and press the Del key.

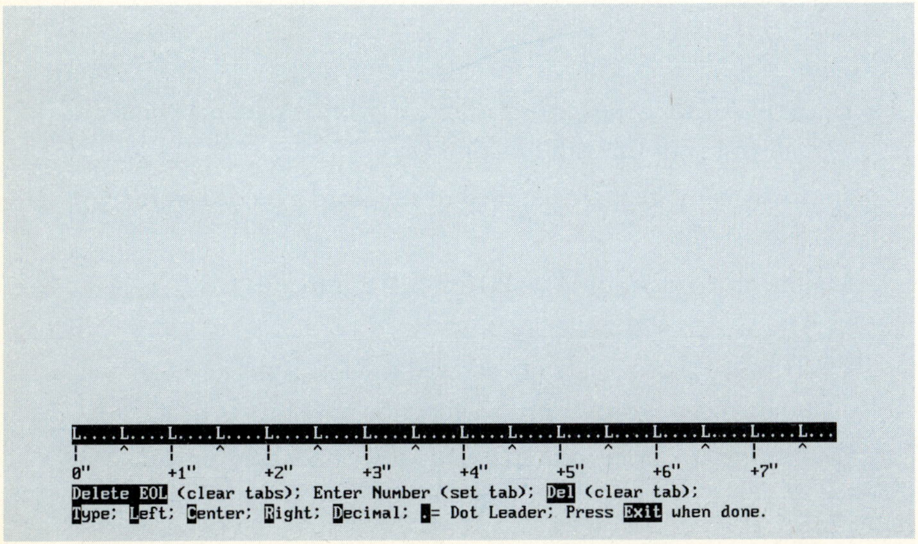

FIGURE 14.3

The WordPerfect 5.1 tab ruler lets you set new tabs and delete old ones.

```
L...L...L...L...L...L...L...L...L...L...L...L...L...L...L...L.
0"       +1"       +2"       +3"       +4"       +5"       +6"       +7"
Delete EOL (clear tabs); Enter Number (set tab); Del (clear tab);
Type: Left; Center; Right; Decimal; .= Dot Leader; Press Exit when done.
```

4. Press the Exit key ($\boxed{\text{F7}}$) twice to return to the edit screen when you have set your tabs.

In addition to setting tabs, you can also use the Line Format menu to change line spacing.

Changing Line Spacing

You can space lines with WordPerfect 5.1 by using the Line menu, as shown in Figure 14.2. To change line spacing, follow these steps:

1. Press $\boxed{\text{Shift}}$-$\boxed{\text{F8}}$.
2. Keyboard **1** to select the Line option.
3. Keyboard **6** to select the Line Spacing option.
4. Keyboard the spacing that you want and press $\boxed{\text{Enter}}$. For example, keyboarding **2** will double-space text, keyboarding **3** will triple-space it, and so on.
5. Press the Exit key ($\boxed{\text{F7}}$) to return to the edit screen when you have set your line spacing.

One word of caution about setting new tabs and line spacing: Be sure that the cursor is positioned *before* the text that you want to affect. The reason is that WordPerfect 5.1 places a special "hidden code," containing the new format change, at the cursor. All text before the cursor will not be affected. For example, to set new tabs in the bottom half of a page, place the cursor halfway down the page, then change the tabs. Only the text positioned after the cursor will be affected.

Remember that if you ever enter a command by mistake, or if a menu appears on the screen that you do not expect, press the Cancel key ($\boxed{\text{F1}}$), and the program will return to where it was before you made the command.

Review

1. Approximately how many different WordPerfect 5.1 commands can you perform with function keys?
2. How many steps are required to keyboard a bolded word? List these steps.
3. The three kinds of WordPerfect 5.1 commands are _____, _____, and _____.
4. True or False: You are not allowed to look at the keyboard when you strike a WordPerfect 5.1 function key.
5. List the keystrokes required to double-space a document.

6. To double-space the bottom half of a document, where must the cursor be when you make the format change?

7. To cancel a command, press _____.

Lesson 15 Underlining Text, -, --, F8

Starting WordPerfect 5.1

1. Start WordPerfect 5.1.
2. Place your data disk in drive B, if it is not already there.

Review

```
1. Vic and Jo recognized that the quotations were not itemized.
2. Zenia quickly answered all their questions and left quietly.
3. Ezra apologized to Trixie by sending her a dozen carnations.
```

Keyboarding To strike the - (hyphen), reach up with the little finger of your right hand.

```
4. ;-; ;-; a one-page letter; an up-to-date report; by mid-day;
5. water-repellent fire-resistant tailor-made air-cooled motors

6. may-be mem-o in-dex in-dus-try in-sured in-struc-tions in-to
7. com-put-er un-able re-fuse dis-tri-bu-tion em-ploy-ee mod-el
```

To key the dash (--), strike the hyphen key twice without spacing.

8. A saw, an awl, and a file--these are the only tools we need.
9. Freshmen, sophomores, and juniors--all were invited to come.

10. G. Salzman does all the work--S. Miller gets all the credit.
11. Success--that is all that motivates them. We all need help.

To underline text, press ⌊F8⌋. The underline key (⌊F8⌋) is a toggle. To use it, follow these steps:

1. Press the Underline key (⌊F8⌋) to turn it on.

2. Keyboard the text.

3. Press the Underline key (⌊F8⌋) again to turn it off.

Depending on the kind of display monitor that you have, underlined characters may appear underscored or in a different color.

12. I suggest reading <u>Good Housekeeping</u>. The articles are good.
13. The <u>Boosters</u>, our local community newspaper, is now on sale.

14. A new book, <u>Skiing</u>, is available in paperback at your store.
15. The U.S.S. <u>Nimitz</u> will dock today at Newport News, Virginia.

Practice

16. ac-count-ing in-de-pend-ent neigh-bor-hood in-sist de-pos-it
17. grad-u-ate in-come fi-nance fold-er fur-ni-ture gov-ern-ment

18. in-ven-to-ry jour-nal ledg-er let-ter man-age-ment man-ag-er
19. guar-an-tee head-quar-ters i-de-a i-den-ti-fi-ca-tion hu-man

20. ec-o-nom-ic fa-cil-i-ty en-ve-lopes em-ploy-ment e-quip-ment
21. a well-known doctor; a two-week trip; an eight-liter bottle;

22. high-priced goods; a pay-as-you-go plan; a self-made person;
23. a part-time job; short-term loans; a once-in-a-lifetime job;

24. Send me the follow-up reports. Please mail them by Tuesday.
25. I think one-half of the payment is due the following Monday.

26. I need directions for doing a top-quality paint job at home.
27. Can you give me step-by-step instructions on motor tune-ups?

28. What should one consider when purchasing a wood-frame house?
29. Bring a typewriter, pencil, and paper--that is all you need.

Skill Checks

```
30.  Now our appliances--microwave ovens and toasters--will sell.
31.  Typical French titles for women are Madame and Mademoiselle.
32.  The words ac-count-ing, ledg-er, and i-de-a are to be keyed.
```

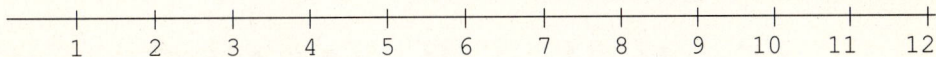

```
     +----+----+----+----+----+----+----+----+----+----+----+
     1    2    3    4    5    6    7    8    9   10   11   12
```

wpm in one-minute timing

Underline Practice

Underline the words where shown.

```
Please remember to watch your head.
She read War and Peace by Leo Tolstoy.
They had to talk to everybody that night.
The label read: Warning.
Watership Down is a great story.
Leave nothing to chance and everything to planning.
```

Underline the titles where shown.

```
They read The Catcher in the Rye, Seymour:  An Introduction,
and Franny and Zooey, by J. D. Salinger.

After finishing Nine Stories, the class decided that Salinger
was a fine American writer.
```

Saving the Lesson

To save the lesson, follow these steps:

1. Press the Save key (F10).
2. Keyboard the name B:LESSON15, then press Enter.

Printing the Lesson

To print the lesson, follow these steps:

1. Use the Print command (Shift-F7).
2. Keyboard 1 to print the document.

Exiting
WordPerfect 5.1

To end the program, follow these steps:

1. Press the Exit key ($\boxed{\text{F7}}$).

2. Keyboard **N**. You have already saved the document.

3. Keyboard **Y** to leave the program.

Lesson 16   Keyboarding in All Capitals:

$\boxed{\text{CapsLock}}$, $\boxed{\text{Tab}}$, :

Starting
WordPerfect 5.1

1. Start WordPerfect 5.1.

2. Place your data disk in drive B, if it is not already there.

Review

1. I told Steve to buy <u>The Wall Street Journal</u> on his way home.
2. The young, middle-aged, and old--they are all oil consumers.
3. hos-pi-tal-i-za-tion or-gan-i-za-tion ques-tion-naire quo-ta

Keyboarding   To key the : (colon), use the left $\boxed{\text{Shift}}$ key and strike the ; (semicolon) key.

4. ;: ;: :: Please bring the following: bread, milk, and eggs.
5. The months of the meetings are: May, October, and November.
6. Three courses are required: botany, biology, and chemistry.
7. The home has many features: a fireplace, a den, and a pool.

Use the CapsLock key to keyboard all capitals. The CapsLock key is a toggle. To use it, follow these steps:

1. Press the CapsLock key to turn it on.
2. Keyboard the word or words.
3. Press the CapsLock key again to turn it off.

8. The sign on the door read: NATIONAL ECONOMIC STAFF MEETING.
9. The major headings in the text were: TRAVEL, MONEY, HEALTH.

10. EDUCATORS and ACCOUNTANTS; DOCTORS and NURSES; BOY and GIRL;
11. The sign at the entrance read: STATE UNIVERSITY OF GEORGIA.

The Tab key is located in the upper-left-hand side of the keyboard. Press the Tab key at the beginning of each paragraph. The Tab key moves the cursor five spaces within your document. WordPerfect 5.1 automatically sets a tab stop every half-inch (5 spaces). Use word wrap except when you need to begin a new paragraph. Your line endings may vary.

12.   Please return the enclosed forms--NOW--so that I may be
able to plan an unforgettable trip. Mail these forms EARLY.
13.   As he may already know, their annual convention will be
held during the last week of October at the Mayflower Hotel.
14.   Pat should enter the display area at the Center through
the gate marked DISPLAY BOOTHS. They will want to see the
following: VHS and Beta receivers, microphones, and radios.
15.   Has Lou joined the Record-a-Month plan? I understand a
weekly issue of their magazine, Records, is available, FREE.

Practice

Double-space paragraphs 16, 17, and 18. To set double-spacing, follow these steps:

1. Press Shift - F8 .
2. Keyboard 1 to select the Line menu.
3. Keyboard 6 to select the Line Spacing option.
4. Keyboard 2 to double-space the document and press Enter .
5. Press F7 to return to the edit screen.

For more detailed instructions on setting line spacing, see Lesson 14. Remember that new line spacing is effective from the cursor forward. Change line spacing to single-space after completing the practice.

16.   There is still time--though not much--to send the order for a season ticket. Send your order to: The University of Florida. Sal will get you the correct address and ZIP code.

17.   David Moser--our former councilman--ordered the hanging of his painting, <u>A Winter Lake</u>. NO SMOKING and DO NOT TOUCH signs were also hung on the showroom wall near the painting.

18.   To celebrate our anniversary, Jo is planning this once-in-a-lifetime offer for all our customers at a SPECIAL RATE.

Skill Checks

In these timings, there are two half-inch paragraph indentations. Subtract one word from your words per minute for each of the paragraph indentations you key.

19.   They did a tip-top job--in fact, the best our professor ever saw. I needed a dozen copies of the articles--quickly.

20.   Note: My copies must be mailed no later than SATURDAY.

```
+    +    +    +    +    +    +    +    +    +    +    +
1    2    3    4    5    6    7    8    9   10   11   12
```

wpm in one-minute timing

Saving the Lesson

To save the lesson, follow these steps:
1. Press the Save key (F10).
2. Keyboard the name B:LESSON16, then press Enter.

Printing the Lesson

To print the lesson, follow these steps:
1. Use the Print command (Shift-F7).
2. Keyboard 1 to print the document.

Exiting WordPerfect 5.1

To end the program, follow these steps:
1. Press the Exit key (F7).
2. Keyboard N. You have already saved the document.
3. Keyboard Y to leave the program.

Lesson 17 Centering a Line with [Shift]-[F6]

**Starting
WordPerfect 5.1**

1. Start WordPerfect 5.1.
2. Place your data disk in drive B, if it is not already there.

Review

Double-space lines 1 through 4. Use word wrap. Change line spacing to single-space after completing the Review.

1.   We made the following purchases: a golf ball, a tennis
2. ball, and a baseball. They were advertised in the Dispatch.
3.   The DESERT CLASSIC championship tennis tournament will be
4. shown live.

Centering a Line

To center a line, use the [Shift]-[F6] command by following these steps:

1. Press [Shift]-[F6].
2. Keyboard the words.
   RESULT: The words appear centered on the line.

Practice

Center each line of this ad.

5.   FOR SALE!
6.   Mountain Creek Home
7.   Decks, Stunning View
8.   Wooded Seclusion
9.   Low Price
10.   Carry Papers

Center each line in the following announcement.

```
11.                  CREATIVE EXHIBIT PLANNERS
12.          is pleased to announce the opening of our new
13.           computerized exhibit development department.
14.         Ms. Marsha Laursen, an exhibit design veteran,
15.              will assist you or your company with:
16.                  o Professional exhibit design
17.                   o Staying within your budget
18.                 o Planning marketing strategies
19.           Stop by our Warner Center offices or give
20.                         Marsha a call.
21.                          EXHIBIT PLACE
22.                Number One, Atlantic Avenue
23.                 Computer City, California
24.                      Free Consultation
```

To spread-center a line of text for greater emphasis, follow these steps:

1. Use the Center command ($\boxed{\text{Shift}}$-$\boxed{\text{F6}}$).

2. Keyboard the text, leaving one space between letters and three spaces between words.

```
25.              U G L Y   T I E   C O N T E S T !
26.                   S I G N - U P   N O W !
```

Double-space lines 27–32.

```
27. The power of association through the sense of smell is a
28. factor that can be exploited in an exhibit. A scent of pine
29. at a logging exhibit adds much, as does a scent of roses at a
30. perfume exhibit. It is well-known that the smell of a new
31. car has sold many customers. Introducing the characteristic
32. smell of an industry can add authenticity to any exhibit.
```

Saving the Lesson

To save the lesson, follow these steps:

1. Press the Save key ($\boxed{\text{F10}}$).

2. Keyboard the name B:LESSON17, then press $\boxed{\text{Enter}}$.

Printing the Lesson	To print the lesson, follow these steps:
	1. Use the Print command (Shift - F7).
	2. Keyboard **1** to print the document.

Exiting WordPerfect 5.1	To end the program, follow these steps:
	1. Press the Exit key (F7).
	2. Keyboard **N**. You have already saved the document.
	3. Keyboard **Y** to leave the program.

Lesson 18   Indenting a Paragraph with F4

Starting WordPerfect 5.1	**1.** Start WordPerfect 5.1.
	2. Place your data disk in drive B, if it is not already there.

Review

```
                    Bug Eating Contest
 1.                    Memorial Park
 2.                 Saturday, Labor Day
 3.
```

Setting the Tab Key	Set a tab every 1.5" (15 spaces) from the left margin. To set tabs, follow these steps:
	1. Press Shift - F8 .

2. Keyboard **1**.

3. Keyboard **8**.

4. Move the cursor to each tab that you want to delete, and press [Del].

5. Move the cursor to each place on the ruler where you want a tab to appear, and keyboard **L**.

6. Press [F7] twice to return to the edit screen.

For more detailed instructions for setting tabs, see Lesson 14. Remember that the new tab format change is effective from the cursor forward.

Keyboard lines 4–16 below by pressing the [Tab] key after each word.

```
 4. Alabama        Alaska         Arizona        Arkansas
 5. California     Colorado       Connecticut    Delaware
 6. Florida        Georgia        Guam           Hawaii
 7. Idaho          Illinois       Indiana        Iowa
 8. Kansas         Kentucky       Louisiana      Maine
 9. Maryland       Massachusetts  Michigan       Minnesota
10. Mississippi    Missouri       Montana        Nebraska
11. Nevada         New Hampshire  New Jersey     New Mexico
12. New York       N. Carolina    North Dakota   Ohio
13. Oklahoma       Oregon         Pennsylvania   Puerto Rico
14. Rhode Island   S. Carolina    South Dakota   Tennessee
15. Texas          Utah           Vermont        Virgin Islands
16. Virginia       Washington     W. Virginia    Wisconsin
```

Using the Indent Key [F4]

WordPerfect 5.1's indent key ([F4]) allows you to move every line of a paragraph to a tab stop. Look at the following example:

```
This paragraph was keyboarded using the Indent key
to move the cursor to position 2" before entering
text. As opposed to the Tab key, which indents the
first line of a paragraph half-an-inch (five
spaces), the Indent key moves every line of the
paragraph to the tab stop.
```

To use the Indent key ([F4]), simply press it. Each time you press it, the cursor moves to the next tab stop, which will be your new left margin.

Indent lines 17–24 at position 2.5" by using the [F4] key. Use word wrap.

```
17.
18.       All good exhibits stimulate more than one sense at
19.       once. When working together, sight, sound, touch,
          smell, and taste are the best sales tools we have.
```

20.
21.
22.
23.

```
The Metropol displays its superb collection of
gems and jewels in a large exhibition hall by
placing them in a series of sparkling and velvet-
lined display cases.
```

Reset tabs to every 1" (10 spaces). Indent the material below at position 2" with the F4 key. Use word wrap. Remember that new tabs are effective from the cursor forward.

24.
25.
26.

```
Consider the "fiddle factor."  Engineers and
technicians love to touch equipment and examine parts
minutely.
```

Saving the Lesson

To save the lesson, follow these steps:
1. Press the Save key (F10).
2. Keyboard the name B:LESSON18, then press Enter.

Printing the Lesson

To print the lesson, follow these steps:
1. Use the Print command (Shift - F7).
2. Keyboard 1 to print the document.

Exiting WordPerfect 5.1

To end the program, follow these steps:
1. Press the Exit key (F7).
2. Keyboard N. You have already saved the document.
3. Keyboard Y to leave the program.

Lesson 19   Bolding Text with $\boxed{\text{F6}}$

| Esc | | F1 | F2 | F3 | F4 | | F5 | **F6** | F7 | F8 | | F9 | F10 | F11 | F12 |

Keyboard diagram

Starting WordPerfect 5.1

1. Start WordPerfect 5.1.
2. Place your data disk in drive B, if it is not already there.

Review

Indent to position 2". Use word wrap.

1.
2.
3.
4.
```
There are five keys to trade show success:  set
specific objectives, construct a sales scenario,
prepare an exhibit that augments the sales plan, train
your staff, and follow up on leads.
```

Using the Bold Key $\boxed{\text{F6}}$

To bold text, press $\boxed{\text{F6}}$. The Bold key is a toggle. To use it, follow these steps:

1. Press the Bold key ($\boxed{\text{F6}}$) to turn it on.
2. Keyboard the text.
3. Press the Bold key ($\boxed{\text{F6}}$) again to turn it off.

Depending on the kind of computer screen you have, the bolded characters may appear highlighted on the screen or they may appear in a different color.

Bold each person's title in the following list. Leave two blank lines between each line of text.

5. **President,** Ken Tanaka

6. **Director of Marketing,** Ellen Nasus

7. **Director of Design,** Marsha Laursen

8. **Director of Operations,** Rick Olson

9. **Director of Public Relations,** Regena Mitchell

10. **Administrative Manager,** Michelle Strongman

Practice

Spread center the title. Indent lines 12–15 to position 1.5". Underline, bold, and capitalize the words shown. Use word wrap.

```
11.              M O V I E   R E V I E W
12.       What made Raiders of the Lost Ark so exciting was
13.       that HARRISON FORD seemed just as surprised as the
14.       audience at the story and yet capable of
15.       overcoming any obstacle.
```

Double-space lines 16–20, and indent them to position 3". Underline, bold, and capitalize the words shown. Use word wrap.

```
16.       Never had the PIED PIPER seemed so appealing
17.       to the children as when he blew light, brief
18.       notes on his way through the town. One by
19.       one the children left their games and
20.       followed him into the wilderness.
```

Single-space and center lines 21–26. Bold and underline words where shown. Double-space lines where appropriate. Spread-center the heading.

```
21.       A N N U A L   B E N E F I T   C O N C E R T
22.              THE BLUE-RIDGE BLUES BOYS
23.              Saturday, Halloween Night
24.               Gates open at Dusk
25.                   Sylvan Park
26.            Computer City, California
```

Saving the Lesson

To save the lesson, follow these steps:

1. Press the Save key (F10).
2. Keyboard the name B:LESSON19, then press Enter.

Printing the Lesson

To print the lesson, follow these steps:

1. Use the Print command (Shift-F7).
2. Keyboard 1 to print the document.

Exiting WordPerfect 5.1

To end the program, follow these steps:

1. Press the Exit key (F7).
2. Keyboard N. You have already saved the document.
3. Keyboard Y to leave the program.

5

Keyboarding Numbers and Symbols

Lesson 20 New Keys: 1, 2, !, and @

Lessons 20 through 25 discuss numbers and special symbols. While most keyboards have a row of numbers across the top, some keyboards will differ. Symbols, as well as numbers, are not in a standard arrangement on keyboards. Use appropriate fingering for *your* keyboard. Where a symbol appears above a number on the same key, use the [Shift] key to create the symbol. Likewise, if more than one symbol appears on a key, use the [Shift] key to create the upper symbol.

Starting WordPerfect 5.1

1. Start WordPerfect 5.1.
2. Place your data disk in drive B, if it is not already there.

Review

1.
2.
3.

$$\textbf{P A Y D A Y \quad B A S H}$$
Friday Night
<u>BYO</u>

Keyboarding   To strike the number **1**, reach up with the little finger of your left hand.

4. Lee and I purchased 11 gallons of gas. I had 11 cents left.
5. The dates of the next two meetings were June 1 and August 1.
6. Refer to page 11 in your text. The report is due January 1.
7. On the first of May, the board meeting will begin at 11 p.m.

To strike the number **2**, reach up with the third finger of your left hand.

8. s2s s2s We will ship you 21 cases during the next 12 months.
9. I moved to 2112 East 222 St. My old address was 12 Eastway.
10. I typed 21 letters for Sally. She asked me to type 12 more.
11. The next meeting will be held on either June 2 or October 2.

To strike the **!**, press the right [Shift] key and reach up with the third finger of your left hand.

Space twice after an exclamation point at the end of a sentence.

12. No! Charge it! Look out! Do not leave! Stay awake! Yes!
13. Stop cooking! Start running! On your mark! Get set! Now!

14. We won! Great! Jump! Catch the football! Hurry! I lost!
15. Of all things to happen! We did it! Lisa won the big game!

To strike the **@**, press the right [Shift] key and reach up with the third finger of your left hand.

16. I purchased 22 boxes @ 22 cents per box. Ed sold two boxes.
17. Do you know if Ed sold 22 items @ 12 cents or 12 @ 22 cents?

18. I sold 12 pencils @ 2 cents each. We need five or six more.
19. Order 222 packages of paper from Angela @ 2 cents per sheet.

Practice

20. All 11 members are to be present. Two members will be late.
21. My records indicate that 12,111 people attended the concert.

22. He asked for 11 stamps and 12 cards. She mailed only three.
23. Steve asked for 21 volunteers. There were many people here.

24. Janice Richardson bought 11 flags for the party on August 1.
25. Very Good! Watch your driving! Just look at what happened!

26. What a beautiful fall day we had! Make the most if it, too!
27. My new manager ordered 12 hamburgers and 12 orders of fries.

28. At 2 p.m. I must leave the office for home. Please call me!
29. Al knew our customers would pay only 22 cents for this item.

Skill Checks

30. Ray sold 12 bottles @ 22 cents each. Donna bought them all!
31. The invoice read 121 items @ 2 cents each, and 2 @ 21 cents.
32. At 2:21 on May 2, 22 athletes left for Florida on Flight 22.

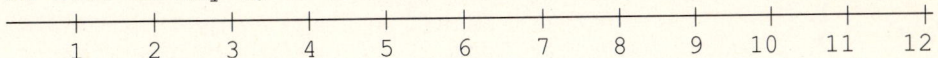

     1   2   3   4   5   6   7   8   9   10   11   12

wpm in one-minute timing

Saving the Lesson

To save the lesson, follow these steps:
1. Press the Save key (F10).
2. Keyboard the name B:LESSON20, then press Enter.

Printing the Lesson

To print the lesson, follow these steps:
1. Use the Print command (Shift-F7).
2. Keyboard 1 to print the document.

Exiting
WordPerfect 5.1

To end the program, follow these steps:

1. Press the Exit key (F7).
2. Keyboard **N**. You have already saved the document.
3. Keyboard **Y** to leave the program.

Lesson 21   New Keys: 3, 4, #, and $

Starting
WordPerfect 5.1

1. Start WordPerfect 5.1.
2. Place your data disk in drive B, if it is not already there.

Review

1. Nan sold 21 pens @ 22 cents each.   I needed to sell 12 more.
2. I am in charge of Room 221; Robert is in charge of Room 222.
3. Throw the ball harder!   Throw the ball faster!   Hit and run!

Keyboarding   To strike the number **3**, reach up with the second finger of your left hand.

4. d3d d3d We expect sales in the amount of 31 million dollars.
5. She was born at Hillcrest Hospital on September 23 at 3 a.m.

6. My sister, at the time, was 3 years 3 months and 3 days old.
7. Steve walked the last mile.   The temperature was 33 degrees.

To strike the number 4, reach up with the first finger of your left hand.

8. f4f f4f What city has the ZIP Code 43211? Joe does not know.
9. When you retrieve your baggage, remember your number: 434.

10. When father arrived in Rome, the temperature was 44 degrees.
11. The temperature at 4 a.m. was 43. By noon the sun came out.

To strike the #, press the right shift key and reach up with the second finger of your left hand.

12. We can offer you #2 pencils. You may want to order several.
13. I noted that check #332 was for 331 items bought on July 31.

14. Three hundred people were at the drawing. Ticket #3213 won.
15. Flight #434 leaves for Rome on May 14 at 4 a.m. Be on time!

To strike the $, press the right shift key and reach up with the first finger of your left hand.

16. When I received the flower bill, I sent a check for $234.44.
17. The clerk at the club made the check for $43 instead of $34.

18. I paid $41 for the coat. This was $14 more than I expected.
19. The ticket for Flight #43 cost $234; last year it cost $144.

Practice

20. It was 32 miles to the nearest rest stop. Tony needed help!
21. My agent suggested we look at page 123 for possible flights.

22. By the time I finished looking, it was 3 p.m.; Sue had left.
23. Al reported that invoice #313 was lost. I issued a new one.

24. Please send us 33 copies of the latest legislative handbook.
25. By 3 p.m. I will be landing in Hawaii. It is my first trip.

26. The odds are 3 to 1 that we will win our first championship.
27. I had to drive 14 miles. When I arrived, it was past 4 p.m.

Skill Checks

28. If you want my address, it is 444 North Star. Please write!
29. Your orders for 3, 4, and 12 dozen roses have been received.

30. I paid $234 for a new suit, $24 for a hat, and $34 for ties.
31. I asked them to buy a #12 brush. They bought a #14 instead.

```
    |   |   |   |   |   |   |   |   |   |   |   |
    1   2   3   4   5   6   7   8   9  10  11  12
```
wpm in one-minute timing

Saving the Lesson

To save the lesson, follow these steps:

1. Press the Save key ([F10]).
2. Keyboard the name B:LESSON21, then press [Enter].

Printing the Lesson

To print the lesson, follow these steps:

1. Use the Print command ([Shift]-[F7]).
2. Keyboard **1** to print the document.

Exiting WordPerfect 5.1

To end the program, follow these steps:

1. Press the Exit key ([F7]).
2. Keyboard **N**. You have already saved the document.
3. Keyboard **Y** to leave the program.

Lesson 22   New Keys: 5, 6, and %

Starting WordPerfect 5.1

1. Start WordPerfect 5.1.
2. Place your data disk in drive B, if it is not already there.

Review

Keep in mind that it is becoming more common to omit periods after **lb** and **oz**.

1. Vanessa and Jimmy bought a 4 lb 3 oz roast that cost $12.42.
2. The object weighed 134 pounds. The line was 12 feet longer.
3. Invoice #41 for $331.42 was lost in shipment on December 23.

Keyboarding

To strike the number 5, reach up with the first finger of your left hand.

4. f5f f5f The typist quoted Diane a rate of five pages for $5.
5. On June 15, Mrs. Santo will celebrate her fortieth birthday.

6. My bank note is due in five months. The payments are $5.55.
7. You can call me from Houston, Texas, for as little as $2.15.

To strike the number 6, reach up with the first finger of your right hand.

8. j6j j6j On February 6, 66 new state employees will be added.
9. Instead of 66, I needed 36. Do you know who made the error?

10. Donald took a $6.6 million gamble when he bought the stocks.
11. The computer listed his age as 61 years 6 months and 6 days.

To strike the % (percent), press the right shift key and reach up with the first finger of your left hand.

12. Discounts range from 15% to 25%. Some offer a 35% discount.
13. The sales chart showed a price reduction of from 15% to 35%.

14. The mortgage interest rates rose from 12% to 15% during May.
15. All five of the office employees received 15% pay increases.

Practice

16. I am enclosing a bill for $545; this will cover my expenses.
17. Are you sure that my sister will not pay more than 65 cents?

18. The ZIP Code is 54545. Minnetonka Mills has a ZIP of 55434.
19. The sale price is $65. We are giving a 16.5% cash discount.

20. At halftime the score was 66 to 55. We won the game by 11.
21. Angie and Diane bought a new radial automobile tire for $65.

22. Review the following figures: 11, 22, 33, 44, 55, 66, 5665.
23. I purchased the following: shoes, $45; socks, $6; ties, $6.

24. These hats--now on sale for $56--were reduced 15% last week.
25. The $65 balance included sales of $16.66, $15.55, and $6.55.

Skill Checks

26. I signed a long-term note for $15,642 at 16% on November 26.
27. We met them at the intersection of State Routes 161 and 315.
28. The prices were listed as follows: wires, $56; covers, $45.

Saving the Lesson

To save the lesson, follow these steps:
1. Press the Save key (F10).
2. Keyboard the name B:LESSON22, then press Enter.

Printing the Lesson

To print the lesson, follow these steps:
1. Use the Print command (Shift-F7).
2. Keyboard 1 to print the document.

Exiting WordPerfect 5.1

To end the program, follow these steps:
1. Press the Exit key (F7).
2. Keyboard N. You have already saved the document.
3. Keyboard Y to leave the program.

Lesson 23 New Keys: 7, 8, &, and *

Starting WordPerfect 5.1

1. Start WordPerfect 5.1.
2. Place your data disk in drive B, if it is not already there.

Review

1. The invoice showed: a $12 racket, a $63 pad, and a $45 pan.
2. I budgeted advertising at 40% for TV and 60% for newspapers.
3. The assignment was to read Chapter 5, Section 6, pages 1-24.

Keyboarding

To strike the number 7, reach up with the first finger of your right hand.

4. j7j j7j He gave me an extension of 17 days; we need 27 more.
5. I was 17 years old when I started playing major league ball.

6. In 1776, the soldier died at the age of 27; his wife was 17.
7. The number 7 came up 11 times in the 77 games Stacey played.

To strike the number 8, reach up with the second finger of your right hand.

8. k8k k8k Driving a car for 18 hours a day can be very tiring.
9. The college term lasts 18 weeks, but my classes end April 8.

10. Eric had an option to buy the lakeside property in 18 weeks.
11. By 8 a.m. the van should be ready to leave for Williamsburg.

To strike the **&** key, press the left shift key and reach up with the first finger of your right hand.

12. Moser & Stanton are as good an accounting firm as Day & Day.
13. The trial of Disantis & Company should be over by August 17.

14. We will need the data from the case of Hart & Son vs. Moser.
15. I began working with Town & Country, Inc., as a sales agent.

To strike the * key, press the left shift key and reach up with the second finger of your right hand.

16. The asterisk, *, is a symbol used to alert us to a footnote.
17. In 1881 Captain John set sail for America with a crew of 8.*

18. Do you know the R Factor* of the insulation in my apartment?
19. The encyclopedia article was titled "Standard of Living."**

Practice

20. The temperature reading at my lake cottage at 8 a.m. was 78.
21. On pages 57, 67, and 77, the stock quotations are incorrect.

22. I need information for the years 1771, 1774, 1775, and 1778.
23. The Jennings, Olinzock, Young & Thiel Company is a law firm.

24. The best way to get to the freeway is to take Route 77 East.
25. Do you know what the population of Akron, Ohio, was in 1881?

26. On account 87, 85 cents is incorrectly given as their price.
27. Cox & Dun, Inc., offered us a fantastic deal on the new car.

28. On December 18, 17 new employees will be added to the staff.
29. The Maxton & Gregg Company is at 18 North Street in Houston.

Skill Checks

30. Suzanne said the accounts marked with an * are confidential.
31. I suggest you contact Euclid, Mayfield & Lee at 711 East 22.
32. We installed a Model AA* roof fan. The fan cost us $287.58.

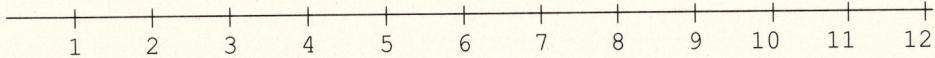

```
  +    +    +    +    +    +    +    +    +    +    +    +
  1    2    3    4    5    6    7    8    9   10   11   12
```

wpm in one-minute timing

Saving the Lesson

To save the lesson, follow these steps:

1. Press the Save key (F10).
2. Keyboard the name B:LESSON23, then press Enter .

Printing the Lesson

To print the lesson, follow these steps:

1. Use the Print command (Shift - F7).
2. Keyboard **1** to print the document.

Exiting WordPerfect 5.1

To end the program, follow these steps:

1. Press the Exit key (F7).
2. Keyboard **N**. You have already saved the document.
3. Keyboard **Y** to leave the program.

Lesson 24 New Keys: 9, 0, (,), and /

Starting
WordPerfect 5.1

1. Start WordPerfect 5.1.
2. Place your data disk in drive B, if it is not already there.

Review

1. The next reference is to: The U.S. Department of Commerce.*
2. Young & Co. charged $78. We decided to call White & Miller.
3. Polly got these facts from Series 35-6, dated June 17, 1881.

Keyboarding   To strike the number **9**, reach up with the third finger of your right hand.

4. 191 191 Should I meet Kelly at 9 a.m.? Or is 9 p.m. better?
5. On November 9, I will be 19 years old. How old will Kim be?

6. Miss Laura Shock now wears a size 9 shoe and a size 9 dress.
7. A normal temperature is 98.6. The package weighs 19 pounds.

To strike the number **0**, reach up with the little finger of your right hand.

8. ;0; ;0; 100 plus 10 equals 110; 100 times 100 equals 10,000.
9. My phone number is 442-1100. Please give me a call tonight.

10. We hope all 20 students will attend the meeting in Room 100.
11. The year 2001 is not too far off. How old will you be then?

To strike the ((left parenthesis), press the left Shift key and reach up with the third finger of your right hand.

To strike the) (right parenthesis), press the left Shift key and reach up with the little finger of your right hand.

12. 1(1 1(1 ;); ;); Eric is sending Mr. Young nine dollars ($9).
13. Your assignment is to study the next chapters (to page 199).

14. In the example given (No. 9), the total amounts are correct.
15. The director authorized a fall party (see minutes of May 9).

LESSON 24 NEW KEYS: 9, 0, (,), AND / 73

To strike the / (slash), reach down with the little finger of your right hand.

16. ;/; ;/; He has 20/20 vision. The interest rate was 14 7/8%.
17. Check the figures for 1981/82. The serial number is AA/000.

18. 3/8 equals .375; 3/4 equals .750; 1 3/8 plus 1 5/8 equals 3.
19. The recipe called for 10 3/4 cups. I added 2 1/3 cups more.

Practice

20. Please send my company 90 copies of your latest sales guide.
21. The financial contract we received had 9 keyboarding errors.

22. The gum cost 20 to 30 cents. We decided to purchase a pack.
23. At noon I will leave for the airport. My gate number is 9A.

24. Flight 999 will arrive at 10 a.m.; it will depart at 11 a.m.
25. Rita lives at 900 Enfield Court; John at 1000 Clubview Blvd.

26. Sue found that 80 to 90 contracts are missing from my files.
27. My new number is 451-1110 (Extension 909). Call me tonight.

28. Bob signed a 36-month note for $9,990 (at 19%) on August 10.
29. All math and science papers are due this month (October 19).

Skill Checks

30. The two sections in the book are (1) practice and (2) tests.
31. The answer to the problem was 10 2/9. My answer was 10 4/9.
32. My best golf scores were 80 on April 19, and 79 on April 20.

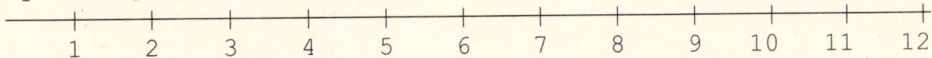

```
  +----+----+----+----+----+----+----+----+----+----+----+
    1    2    3    4    5    6    7    8    9   10   11   12
```
wpm in one-minute timing

Saving the Lesson

To save the lesson, follow these steps:

1. Press the Save key (F10).
2. Keyboard the name B:LESSON24, then press Enter.

Printing the Lesson

To print the lesson, follow these steps:

1. Use the Print command ([Shift]-[F7]).
2. Keyboard **1** to print the document.

Exiting
WordPerfect 5.1

To end the program, follow these steps:

1. Press the Exit key ([F7]).
2. Keyboard **N**. You have already saved the document.
3. Keyboard **Y** to leave the program.

Lesson 25   New Keys: ', ", =, and +

Starting
WordPerfect 5.1

1. Start WordPerfect 5.1.
2. Place your data disk in drive B, if it is not already there.

Review

1. The terms for the equipment Rae had shipped were 2/30, n/60.
2. Prepare (as on page 9) a reference page showing the changes.
3. I require a service charge ($20 minimum) on each mail order.

K e y b o a r d i n g

To strike the ' (apostrophe), reach to the right with the little finger of your right hand.

4. ;'; ;'; Dad's watch can't be fixed.   Won't he buy a new one?
5. That's an expensive watch.   You're sure Margo has the money?

6. I'm sure Suzanne's automobile will be ready by four o'clock.
7. You'll be surprised when one o'clock arrives.   It's a party!

To strike the " (quotation), press the left shift key and reach to the right with the little finger of your right hand.

Leave a space outside, not inside, the quotation marks.

8. "Now is the time," Dr. Jones said, "when we must save fuel."
9. "I hope this works," Tom James said. "Don't worry," I said.

10. The sign said, "Think Metric!" Perhaps I should study more.
11. I want Jo to read "Buying Used Cars." I'll send Di a copy.

To strike the = (equals symbol), reach up with the little finger of your right hand.

To strike the + (plus symbol), press the left shift key and reach up with the little finger of your right hand.

12. The graffiti overhead said, "Martha + Hank = Eternal Love."
13. 43 + 119 = 162 appeared on the paper to everyone's surprise.

14. MaryAnne asked for a proof that the numbers 104 + 215 = 319.
15. Whether or not 43 + 252 = 295 was thrown open to discussion.

Practice

16. The class of '80 will meet at Tony's Pizza House on June 19.
17. Did he or didn't he?   Had he or hadn't he?   She has done it.

18. I'd let them know soon.   Let's call them.   Here's the phone.
19. I'll tell her we've left and we're on our way.   What's that?

20. He's the owner.   We'd better ask for help before they close.
21. Shall we go to the men's department first?   I'll call Anita.

22. Please let me know if this book is Nan's, Linda's, or Sue's.
23. I climbed to the peak and couldn't ski down until it snowed.

```
24.  The store sold out of children's shoes but still had shirts.
25.  Another article for Ed to read is "Men's & Women's Apparel."

26.  Let's all sign "Happy Anniversary" to Mr. and Mrs. Fedrico.
27.  "Great!" he exclaimed when we told him his office was ready.

28.  "Isn't this your special for the day?" Kay asked her waiter.
29.  "You can start keyboarding," she said, "when I say 'Begin.'"
```

Skill Checks

```
30.  "Please write 50 + 50 = 100 in your notebook," Mr. Lee said.
31.  The nurse said, "You need a physical examination next week."
32.  I won't pay for the ski trip to Colorado.  Can't Norman pay?
```
```
    +   +   +   +   +   +   +   +   +   +   +   +
    1   2   3   4   5   6   7   8   9   10  11  12
```
wpm in one-minute timing

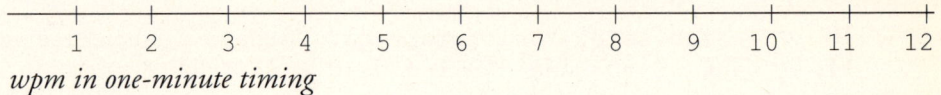

Saving the Lesson

To save the lesson, follow these steps:

1. Press the Save key ([F10]).
2. Keyboard the name B:LESSON25, then press [Enter].

Printing the Lesson

To print the lesson, follow these steps:

1. Use the Print command ([Shift]-[F7]).
2. Keyboard **1** to print the document.

Exiting WordPerfect 5.1

To end the program, follow these steps:

1. Press the Exit key ([F7]).
2. Keyboard **N**. You have already saved the document.
3. Keyboard **Y** to leave the program.

If you have completed all the lessons up to this point, you will be glad to know that you have had experience in using the entire keyboard and its basic features. From this point on, study the material that is most suited to your needs.

Lesson 26 The Numeric Keypad and Right-Aligned Tabs

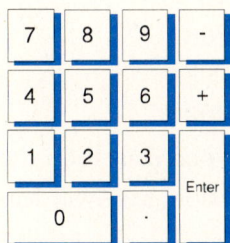

When you keyboarded Lessons 20–24, you probably found it difficult to stretch your fingers between the letters in the home row and the numbers in the top row. For the same reason, professionals who key many numbers usually use a numeric keypad. The numeric keypad on a microcomputer is similar to the kind found on a ten-key calculator, except that the one on the microcomputer may also include a period, a comma, a hyphen, and an Enter key.

Using the Numeric Keypad Home Position

Like the keyboard, the numeric keypad has a home position. The home position is **4**, **5**, **6**, with the index finger on the **4**, the middle finger on the **5**, and the ring finger on the **6**.

As with the alphabetic keyboard, using proper fingering increases speed and accuracy. The index finger is used to strike the **1** and **7** keys; the middle finger strikes the **2** and **8** keys; the ring finger strikes the **3** and **9** keys; and the thumb strikes the **0**. You can strike the period and the Enter key using any finger that feels the most comfortable.

To use the numeric keypad on a microcomputer keyboard, the NumLock option must be on. Press the **8** key on your numeric keypad. If the number **8** appears on the screen, NumLock is on. If nothing happens, or if the cursor moves up one line, press the NumLock key once to activate the numeric keypad.

Setting Right-Aligned Tabs: Entering Columns of Numbers

The easiest way to enter columns of numbers is to set *right-aligned* tabs for each column. So far, you have used *left-aligned* tabs for columns (the **L** on the tab ruler means **left-aligned**).

Right-aligned tabs align numbers on the right edge, such as in the following list of numbers:

200

97

3298

To set right tabs, keyboard an **R** on the tab ruler where you want the tab. In the following lesson, you will learn in detail how to set right-aligned tabs.

Starting WordPerfect 5.1

1. Start WordPerfect 5.1.

2. Place your data disk in drive B, if it is not already there.

3. Press Shift - F8.

4. Keyboard **1** to select the Line option.

5. Keyboard **8** to select the Tab option.

6. Delete all tab settings by moving the cursor with the → key to each **L** and pressing Del.

7. Move the cursor to position 1" and keyboard an **R**.
   RESULT: **R** appears on the ruler line.

8. Place an **R** at positions 1", 2", 3", 4", 5", 6", and 7".

9. Press the Exit key (F7) twice to return to the edit screen.

10. Enter the following data by tabbing to each column; that is, keyboard tab 4, tab 5, tab 6, and so on. When you reach the end of the row, press Enter on the numeric keypad to continue to the next row. If you make a mistake and want to use the Del key or move the cursor, you will need to turn NumLock off by pressing NumLock once. (If you have an enhanced keyboard, use the Del key and cursor movement keys between the alphabet keys and the numeric keypad.)

Home Row	4	5	6	4	5	6
Keys	44	55	66	44	55	66
	66	55	44	66	55	44
	444	555	666	444	555	666
	456	654	564	465	546	645
	4444	5555	6666	4565	6454	6546
	6464	5656	5454	4545	4646	6565

Bottom	1	2	3	1	2	3
Row Keys	11	22	33	11	22	33
	33	22	11	33	22	11
	111	222	333	111	222	333
	123	321	231	132	213	312
	1111	2222	3333	1232	3121	3213
	3131	2323	2121	1212	1313	3232
Top Row	7	8	9	7	8	9
Keys	77	88	99	77	88	99
	99	88	77	99	88	77
	777	888	999	777	888	999
	789	987	897	798	879	978
	7777	8888	9999	7898	9787	9879
	9797	8989	8787	7878	7979	9898
Index	4	1	7	4	1	7
Finger Keys	44	11	77	44	11	77
	11	44	77	77	44	11
	111	444	777	111	444	777
	147	741	714	417	471	174
	1111	4444	7777	1474	4741	7417
	1741	7471	1774	4117	7147	4714
Middle	5	2	8	5	2	8
Finger Keys	55	22	88	55	22	88
	22	55	88	88	55	22
	222	555	888	222	555	888
	258	852	825	528	582	285
	2222	5555	8888	2585	5852	8528
	2852	8582	2885	5228	8258	5825
Ring	6	3	9	6	3	9
Finger Keys	66	33	99	66	33	99
	33	66	99	99	66	33
	333	666	999	333	666	999
	369	963	936	639	693	396
	3333	6666	9999	3696	6963	9639
	3963	9693	3996	6339	9369	6936

Thumb Key	0	1	0	2	0	3
	40	50	60	70	80	90
	00	01	02	03	04	05
	060	070	080	090	100	200
	300	400	500	600	700	800
	1000	2000	3000	4000	5000	6000
	7000	8000	9000	9040	5070	3200

Combination	1234	4321	5678	8765	9090	1357
of Keys	2468	8642	7531	9012	1256	7834
	1029	3847	5160	9102	3481	5387
	13579	24680	12568	34790	10293	48576
	33241	77509	59866	13228	19485	12348
	84732	49298	12948	42947	70005	35578
	309485	483947	293484	22343	009873	293884
	6778859	6857489	9948328	767532	8928176	2283910
	#36,590	#54,683	#99,073	#11,765	#10,984	#22,804
	$405.67	$593.77	$100.26	$848.38	$979.02	$645.88
	26.4%	19.5%	37.8%	80.2%	91.3%	45.6%
	(247)	(806)	(135)	(920)	(893)	(415)

The United States Post Office has recommended that businesses use a nine-digit ZIP code to speed the delivery of mail. Keyboard the following ZIP codes. Do not use tabs; simply leave one space between each code. Use the hyphen on the numeric keypad.

```
55124-3658 30182-9063 27234-4127 76515-8588 24620-5590

02769-3322 54405-8092 98004-5766 00916-1247 78410-8324

28804-5356 63116-9008 16862-4633 02916-9876 96719-6544
```

Saving the Lesson

To save the lesson, follow these steps:

1. Press the Save key ([F10]).
2. Keyboard the name B:LESSON26, then press [Enter].

Printing the Lesson

To print the lesson, follow these steps:

1. Use the Print command (Shift - F7).
2. Keyboard **1** to print the document.

*Exiting
WordPerfect 5.1*

To end the program, follow these steps:

1. Press the Exit key (F7).
2. Keyboard **N**. You have already saved the document.
3. Keyboard **Y** to leave the program.

6

Practicing Keystrokes

Lesson 27   Alphabetic Keyboard Review

This lesson contains several drills for increasing your keyboarding skill. The first two drills—Letter Sequence Drills and Alphabetic Sentence Drills—will give you practice in keying every letter of the alphabet and some combinations of letters.

Three other drills—Stroke Refinement Practice, Progressive Practice on the Alphabet, and Progressive Practice on Numbers and Symbols— will help you develop speed and accuracy. The Stroke Refinement Drills will give you practice in keyboarding some difficult letter combinations. The Progressive Practice Drills will help you develop dexterity in keyboarding the alphabet, numbers, and symbols.

Contrary to what you might expect, developing keyboarding skill depends on learning combinations of letters, not on learning individual letters. To practice each letter, two sets of drills are provided: Letter Sequence Drills and Alphabetic Sentence Drills.

Letter Sequence Drills

In the first set of drills, the Letter Sequence Drills, the featured letter is followed by each letter of the alphabet, when that letter combination exists in English. (Note that some of the words are very obscure.)

Keyboard each line so that you will become familiar with common (and some not-so common) letter combinations. Keyboard at a comfortable speed—not so quickly that you make a lot of errors, but not too slowly. If you sense that you have made an error, immediately repeat the word. Word groups are separated by extra line spacing. For each group of words, use word wrap to allow the cursor to move automatically to the next line.

Do not spend more than ten minutes at a time on this drill. Alternate with Alphabetic Sentence Drills.

a   aardwolf, able, account, ad, aegis, after, age, ahead, aid, ajar, akin, all, am, an, aorta, appear, aqua, are, as, at, auto, average, away, ax, aye, azure

aardvark, back call, date, each, fact, gas, had, pediatric, jazz, karate, labor, machine, name, oak, page, Qatar, rate, same, take, actual, valuable, want, xanthic, yard, zap

b   back, jobber, subcommittee, subdivide, be, subgroup, subhead, binder, object, bk., blank, submit, bn., board, bp., bring, absence, debt, build, obviously, bwana, bx., by

about, ribbon, Macbeth, handbook, baseball, offbeat, ragbag, neighbor, contribute, workbook, albums, ambulance, unbend, obtain, raspberry, carbon, husband, football, club, vb., jawbone, oxblood, anybody, Uzbeg

c   call, cb, accept, cd., ceiling, cf., cg., chair, circuit, truck, claim, cm, Cnidus, coal, Macpherson, acquaint, crest, cs., victory, cultural, cwt, cycle, czar

acid, bobcat, accent, redcap, echo, offcenter, dogcatcher, ashcan, ice, jct., malcontent, McCue, violence, occasion, tuberculosis, school, watch, voucher, showcase, exceed

d   daily, handbook, broadcast, diddle, deal, edge, dhole, dial, Djakarta, dk., friendly, dm, dn., do, standpoint, headquarters, drawings, friends, width, due, inadvertently, dwarf, dynamite, dz.

ad, subdue, McDonald, odd, edition, serfdom, Baghdad, birthday, idea, breakdown, child, dumdum, end, body, update, forward, wisdom, outdo, include, Blvd., powder, everybody, Yazd

e   each, ebb, economical, education, need, efficient, egg, eh, either, eject, leek, electric, emerge, enable, eon, epic, equal, error, especially, etc., euphoria, evaluate, ewe, exact, eyes, Ezra

aerial, be, ceiling, deal, agree, feat, gene, head, applies, subject, keep, lead, me, near, foe, peace, reach, sea, team, continue, very, we, deluxe, year, dozen

f   face, fear, affect, fiber, fjord, Kafka, flat, foil, frame,
         proofs, aircraft, fuel, verify

         affairs, subfreezing, McFall, goldfish, effort, office,
         bagful, faithfully, if, thankful, behalf, comfort, unfix,
         off, helpful, wonderful, transformer, thoughtfulness, suffer,
         awful, Oxford, joyful

g   gas, dogberry, dogcart, Gdansk, general, meaningful,
         suggest, freight, gift, Gk., glad, gm., foreign, go,
         dogpatch, grade, songs, strength, guarantee, Gwyn, gypsum

         age, subgrade, McGee, knowledge, egg, Afghanistan, struggle,
         flashgun, high, jg, backgammon, bulge, listing, dog, popgun,
         forget, misguide, catgut, rug, lawgiver, playgoer

h   habit, Hb, forthcoming, withdraw, he, truthful, hg.,
         withholding, hidden, hl, asthma, hold, hp, hr., paths,
         flight, hug, Hwang Hai, hydroelectric, Hz

         ahead, subhuman, chair, childhood, behalf, offhanded, sighs,
         withhold, hardihood, Jhansi, backhanded, girlhood, Amhara,
         Arnhem, oh, phase, perhaps, shall, than, uhlan, what, exhale,
         policyholder

i   piano, exhibit, ice, idea, field, if, figure, skiing, ikon,
         ill, immediate, inasmuch, caption, slip, unique, iron,
         issue, it, medium, give, Iwo Jima, six, Iyar, size

         aid, bid, circle, difference, either, fighting, give, high,
         Hawaii, jingle, kindly, lie, might, night, oil, picture,
         Iraqi, rights, side, ticket, ruin, visit, will, taxi, yield,
         grazing

j   jazz, jct., project, jg, jib, Jl., job, jr., just, Jy.

         major, subject, adjustment, rejected, fjeld, logjam,
         highjack, demijohn, jigger, blackjack, killjoy,
         circumjacent, enjoy, projects, flapjack, Marjorie, disjoin,
         bootjack, hallelujah

k   package, breakdown, keep, breakfast, background, khaki, kid,
         bookkeeping, kleenex, embankment, know, kodak, stockpile,
         Kris, backs, pickup, sky

         break, acknowledge, handkerchief, creek, Kafka, Bangkok,
         Oshkosh, strike, bookkeeper, bulk, mkt., bank, book,
         pumpkin, clerk, ask, catkin, Luke, gawk, tyke

l

label, lb., build, lead, half, light, milk, yellow, almost, load, appeals, although, luck, themselves, reply

all, black, claim, handle, electric, flat, glad, pamphlet, ill, Jl., anklet, small, Hamlet, suddenly, old, place, airlines, sleep, slightly, ultimate, Vladivostok, newly, laxly, Sheryl, sizzle

m

made, lumber, McKay, Md, me, mfg., mg, mhometer, might, mkt., firmly, recommend, mnemonic, monk, lamp, Mr., systems, Mt. Rainier, much, Mv, Mw, Mx, my

am, submit, chacma, badman, emergency, Kauffman, stigma, asthma, immediate, workmanship, helm, ammunition, inmost, omitted, topmost, storm, small, nutmeg, sum, sawmill, Axminster carpet, payment

n

name, unbutton, agency, and, hear, confirm, being, inherit, nice, enjoy, bank, only, abandonment, manner, no, manpower, banquet, unreal, means, want, number, convenience, meanwhile, anxious, nylon, enzyme

an, abnegate, picnic, didn't, end, deafness, sigh, technic, in, known, illness, column, annual, one, hypnotize, return, snakes, witness, unit, down, laxness, shyness

o

oak, objectives, occur, odd, does, off, recognize, oh, oil, project, okay, old, omitted, on, food, open, croquet, or, cost, other, our, over, own, proxy, boys, frozen

aorta, board, come, do, people, follow, go, hold, opinion, job, beckon, load, model, none, noon, point, road, so, to, quorum, volume, woman, buxom, you, amazon

p

page, upbeat, popcorn, update, peace, pfenning, pg., phase, pick, upkeep, place, shipment, pneumonia, point, appear, prefer, psychology, kept, purchase, Pvt., upward, expand, pygmy

apply, subpoena, McPeak, standpoint, reply, halfpace, magpie, hp., receipt, pulpit, prompt, unpaid, open, appeal, sharp, space, output, up, cowpea, expense, type

q

aquatic, acquaint, headquarters, equal, earthquake, unique, kumquat, inquiry, loquacious, parquet, squad, quality, exquisite *r*   radio, carbon, purchase, order, read, perfect, large, perhaps, right, lumberjack, work, early, term, learn, road, corporation, error, first, department, run, survey, forward, every

are, branch, credit, drop, errors, free, grade, through, iron, jr., Akron, already, Mr., enroll, or, practice, qr., worry, misrepresent, trade, urge, Louvre, write, payroll, Ezra

s   safe, busboy, school, wisdom, sea, satisfy, Sgt., shall, side, musjid, skill, slip, small, snow, so, space, square, disregard, less, staff, subject, svelte, sweets, system

as, jobs, clinics, words, estimate, offset, brings, lengths, is, works, bills, forms, plans, cost, psychology, yours, session, agents, us, vs., views, myself, buzzsaw

t   tab, textbooks, switch, tell, thoughtful, mortgage, than, tie, catkin, gentlemen, department, partner, to, output, trade, outside, written, turn, two, typist, pretzel

at, debt, act, width, etc., after, length, right, it, blacktop, results, boomtown, into, total, accept, qt., certain, staff, better, utility, Vt., growth, next, anything, Aztec

u   annual, club, such, student, due, manufacturing, suggest, Fuhrer, guide, rebuke, could, number, unable, continuous, up, urge, us, utmost, vacuum, juvenile, deluxe, buy

audit, but, cut, due, lieu, fuel, gun, human, gymnasium, judge, pickup, lunch, such, number, out, pull, question, runs, such, turns, vacuums, vulture, swung, sexual, yucca, zucchini

v   van, vb., vehicle, via, Pavlov, volume, Chevrolet, vs., Vt., vulture, revved, bevy

average, obvious, advise, even, Nashville, ivory, Rockville, solved, circumvent, invest, over, Pvt., service, svelte, outvoted, juvenile, flivver, Bronxville, rendezvous

w   wage, crowbar, crowd, we, lowfat, what, wide, wk., acknowledges, endowments, downtown, women, wp., write, bylaws, growth, followup, powwow, lawyer

award, subway, cwm, dwelling, crew, halfway, dogwatch,
highway, handiwork, awkwardly, always, Cromwell,
commonwealth, owes, upwards, airways, switched, two, Kuwait,
glowworms, Maxwell, anyway

x   example, oxbow, excuse, xd, taxes, Oxford, exhaust,
approximately, axle, Xn., exotic, inexpensive, xr, exsert,
textbooks, sexual, xw, Foxx, proxy

axles, bxg, extras, six, calxes, larynx, boxes, pxt., Marx,
deluxe, Exxon, pyxie

y   yard, maybe, psychiatric, everyday, year, playful,
playground, policyholders, yield, bylaws, employment,
Evelyn, you, types, payroll, system, anything, Yule, anyway,
analyze

away, by, cycle, already, eyes, clarify, gypsum, why, sky,
apply, myself, anybody, boy, copy, advisory, symbol, type,
buy, heavy, lawyer, proxy, lazy

z   hazard, zeal, authorizing, gizmo, zoo, zucchini,
rendezvous, zymometer, gizzard

amazing, subzone, eczema, adz, dozen, freeze, sizes, Balzac,
frenzy, dozens, Leipzig, Tarzan, blitz, fuze, frowzy,
analyzed, razzmatazz

Alphabetic Sentence Drills

In the next series of drills, the Alphabetic Sentence Drills, each of the numbered groups contains every letter of the alphabet. Use the practice conditions explained for the preceding "Letter Sequence Drills" section. If you wish to measure your performance, note that each line is 12 wpm for one-minute timings. Use the scale at the end of the Alphabetic Sentence Drills to determine the wpm for partial lines. After ten minutes of practice, return to the "Letter Sequence Drills" section.

1. Will Ginger and Suzanne pick up the five tickets for my jazz
concert by Monday? Yes, Quint has put them in a yellow box.

2. Gil requested that the orchestra play a waltz or fox trot as
its next number. I was amazed when Jack asked Bev to dance.

3. Flo and Jo recognized that the quotations were not itemized.
I asked P. V. Bixby to check the weekly computer statements.

4. The accountants quickly answered all their questions. Zenia and Jovia expected a simplified analysis of the budget data.

5. Felix got to the airport too late to see the jumbo jet land. But he did see Wyn's cargo of zircons being removed quickly.

6. Jim ordered a sixteen oz. steak with baked potato and salad. Glyn decided on quiche and ordered a carafe of vintage wine.

7. The spelling list contained the following words: authorize, acknowledgment, banquet, delivery, satisfactory, mix, enjoy.

8. When Jan Zyg bought her new car, she quoted the newspaper ad hailing the Model XK-1 as the most advanced car of the year.

9. Computer programming can be an appropriate career choice for anyone who qualifies. Check your daily papers for a listing of jobs. You can realize a very rewarding and exciting job.

10. As Viva and Jane quietly left the camp by the lake, they saw two zebras grazing near a waterhole. Both were very excited and made a hasty trip back to the cabin, where they told Mel.

11. The instructor asked us to define the following terms: job, merger, profit, quota, proxy, account, voucher, withholding, welfare, and amortized. We were able to define all but two.

12. Our family took a trip to the zoo. We saw many animals. Vi loved the chimpanzees and zebras. Monique enjoyed seeing the walrus, wolf, and yak. Rose and I also liked seeing a lynx.

13. Zak and Vern were anxious to plan the sales trip. They took a company plane and flew to Jean's headquarters on Thursday. By the end of the second day, Zak was ready to go back home.

14. Do you know what form of exercise is in vogue today? It's a form of physical activity that's not only fun but important to your health. It's called walking! Do you take walks? I know Jacqueline does. She and Zak take one every afternoon.

15. Frosty is a West Highland terrier. She can be recognized by her white fur coat and jet black eyes. Occasionally she has to be taken to a vet for an examination. She always quivers when we make these trips. But we still like her as our pet.

```
   +    +    +    +    +    +    +    +    +    +    +    +
   1    2    3    4    5    6    7    8    9   10   11   12
```

wpm in a one-minute timing

Stroke Refinement Practice

Among the more common errors made in keyboarding is the switching of one key with another. One way to decrease the number of such errors is to practice the letters that you switch. There are two such exercises in this drill: the first provides a single line for each pair of commonly switched letters, while the second provides six lines for each pair.

You can keyboard this material at any point during the course after you have learned the keyboard. You may key the drills from the beginning—or, if you are aware of making certain frequent switches, you may practice those specific pairs.

To determine which drills to practice, use the table that follows to locate the combinations that you often switch. For example, suppose that you often switch the B and V letters. Since **8** is the only number common to both B and V, sentence 8 or group 8 would be the one to practice. Each line contains at least four strokes on each of the identified letters.

If you wish to take timings on these lines, note that each line completed in a one-minute timing is equal to 12 words per minute. For each five strokes completed beyond a complete line, add one wpm. If you key 15 strokes more than two lines, you will have keyed 2 x 12 = 24 wpm, plus 15/5 = 3 wpm, for a total of 27 wpm.

Stroke Refinement Drills by Letter and Paragraph

a	4, 14, 30, 36		n	2, 33
b	8, 33, 34		o	3, 11, 25
c	16, 19, 31, 32		p	25
d	6, 10, 16, 18, 23		q	36
e	5, 7, 9, 10, 14, 27, 29		r	1, 7, 24, 26
f	12, 18, 24, 37		s	4, 6, 22, 27, 31, 32, 38
g	12, 20, 28, 34		t	1, 21, 28, 29, 37
h	20		u	13, 17, 26
i	3, 5, 13, 35		v	8, 19
j			w	9, 22
k	15, 23, 35, 38		x	32
l	11, 15		y	17, 21
m	2		z	30

r/t 1. Our corporate headquarters sent us a poor economic forecast.

m/n 2. Both men and women are mentioned in the manpower manuscript.

o/l 3. Automobiles have become very expensive. Will this continue?

a/s 4. I gave my arguments for the alternatives to the businessman.

e/i   **5.**   We deposited five dividend checks in their checking account.

s/d   **6.**   The president had a misunderstanding with his two daughters.

r/e   **7.**   Many representatives of the retail merchants were surprised.

v/b   **8.**   Convertibles are everybody's favorite. Is Bill's available?

w/e   **9.**   We're looking forward to our wonderful weekend in Milwaukee.

d/e   **10.**   We considered corresponding with my friend's four daughters.

o/l   **11.**   I located several loyal volunteers for the holiday luncheon.

f/g   **12.**   Gregg had difficulty finding a fishing resort near his home.

i/u   **13.**   Bruce's supervisors were interested in occupational studies.

a/e   **14.**   The manufacturer misplaced all of our chocolate merchandise.

k/l   **15.**   Al took a weekly walk around the block. It was a quick one.

c/d   **16.**   My recommendation was to include all the Medicare documents.

u/y   **17.**   Naturally, your university can design two community centers.

f/d   **18.**   I had a difference of opinion on Fred's wildlife referendum.

c/v   **19.**   Can he discover productive, cooperative vocational services?

g/h   **20.**   Gregg's stenographers have just completed eighty paragraphs.

y/t   **21.**   Yesterday the warranty expired on Tony's automobile battery.

s/w   **22.**   Wes saw the two wheels turn slowly on the worker's snowplow.

d/k   **23.**   I picked three skilled workers to check the dozen handbooks.

f/r   **24.**   I can forgive her for the first fire but not her second one.

p/o   **25.**   The opera opened with two performances at the state capital.

r/u   **26.**   My youngster's outdoor tour was underway by early afternoon.

s/e   **27.**   Les requested that I wait to revise the salesmen's salaries.

g/t   **28.**   Is Sue still interested in studying real estate legislation?

e/t   **29.**   We visited three trailer parks while traveling in Tennessee.

z/a   **30.**   I bought a dozen jazz magazines. Zelda realized I had them.

s/c   **31.**   Economics, chemistry, and psychology are my college courses.

x/c/s 32.   Alexis expects to be excused from doing excessive exercises.

b/n 33.   The bank clerk balanced the books and recorded the balances.

g/b 34.   The publishing company bought the brokerage firm's building.

i/k 35.   Kris spent the summer working in the hotel kitchen with Kim.

q/a 36.   Quint is questionable as a quarterback. Does Allen qualify?

t/f 37.   This is a beautiful afternoon to watch the aircraft perform.

s/k 38.   The tickets were left at the desk. Kris bought three books.

1. r/t   artist birth carton destroy earth farther great heart import
letter matter neutral operate part quarter rate shirt thirty
travel treatment try turn transport undertake vertical write

Fred read their advertisements on computers and calculators.
The newsletter printers are participating in the promotions.
Approximately thirteen stenographers trained the youngsters.

2. m/n   alumni becoming comment demand economic formation government
human income main means mine moment money months moon moving
name number payment remain swimming timing uniform welcoming

The manufacturer used modern instruments to weigh specimens.
Numerous documents on programming are shipped to our alumni.
My memorandum on contemporary economic problems was missing.

3. o/i   action choice decision education forgive going hoping income
join knowing looking mission nation obtain office oil option
period polio question radio senior topic union voice without

Don chose the senior architect as the recreational director.
The oil company officials unanimously voted for an increase.
I apologize for canceling my event so that I could vacation.

4. a/s   acts as ask aspect assess asset assist assume bags base case
delays ease fast gas has ideas last mass names occasion pass
quarts reasons said sale same say task usual vast wash years

Our administrators are always anxious to arrange for leases.
Susan read in the papers that the negotiations are complete.
There are usually many vacancies in my secretarial seminars.

5. *e/i* abilities being cities denied easier eight either field give
hire items idea joined keeping lies miles nine offices piece
pipe quiet receive science their united variety weight yield
A worthwhile career is computer training. Is Lee qualified?
The superintendent liked my teaching techniques and lessons.
Failure to replace defective tires could lead to a disaster.

6. *s/d* adds beds cards debts ends fields grades heads island judges
kinds leads methods needs orders pads questioned reads roads
said seed skilled towards unused visited wished words yields

The stockholders refused the dividends. I lost the records.
The ladies misplaced the awards. We selected newer designs.
Adjustments should be considered when developing my budgets.

7. *r/e* acre bear care dear erect fare great hear inner jobber large
manner near offer paper quarterly reach real rear red reduce
refer refuse route role secret tear upper very later younger

Recently retired persons prefer reading poetry for pleasure.
Typewriting teachers earn certificates for their experience.
Each of their eight veteran volunteers received recognition.

8. *v/b* above available beaver behavior believes beverages boulevard
convertible everybody favorable objectives observed valuable
believe believed obviously observation objective subdivision

They observed the valuable convertible near the subdivision.
Everybody observed her behavior. Avoid being observed also.
Vic believes in being prepared. Is the objective favorable?

9. *w/e* allowed below crew drew elsewhere few grew however interview
knew lower mower new owe power renew somewhat threw underway
view we week well went were wet wheel when whose wind yellow

The newspaper owner acknowledged ownership of the documents.
We'll renew our twenty contracts. Please allow a few weeks.
Is it worthwhile to award back wages to these seven writers?

10. *d/e* added backed called date deal dear deed done dress edge ends
folder grade held ideal justified killed lad media need owed
pride quoted rider slide tied under visited wonder yesterday

The detailed budget recommendation was delivered on Tuesday.
The judges questioned Dee yesterday. Does she seem worried?
The audience laughed as the friendly clown danced with Dean.

11. o/l   allowed blocks collected dollar enroll follow gallon holiday
involve journal kilowatts load local lodge looked love model
normal only pool role school technology unemployed volt wool

Our college counselor normally consults with our department.
Gasoline and oil can become costly. You may travel by rail.
Let us welcome the officials. She wants to use a telephone.

12. f/g   affecting confusing fig figure filing financing fight figure
flying forget forgive gift golf gulf informing manufacturing
notifying offering performing roofing significant thoughtful

Flying, fishing, golf, and skiing are all gratifying sports.
Please forgive me if Guy's gift is not here. Gen forgot it.
Gail was grateful for the gifts. They were sent by freight.

13. i/u   acquire build causing during equipment fluid genuine housing
include inquired instruct issue junior liquid medium nursing
outfit pickup quick require suit tuition unit visual without

The subcommittee authorized reductions for our universities.
June's druggist discounts subscriptions for union employees.
We should understand that productivity is a universal issue.

14. a/e   able acted advance after age airline area beach chapter dear
each ear ease enable fears great hear instead lead mean near
ocean pages qualified reach sea team unable verbal wear year

This assignment is suitable for technicians and specialists.
The temporary stage is square. Cancel the cheaper cabinets.
Everyday dungarees are economical. Disregard her arguments.

15. k/l   acknowledge blanks clerks folks killed kindly knowledge lack
lakes liked locks looks lock milk outlook quickly remarkable
skilled slack stockpile talked talking walked walking weekly

Karl asked Kelly to take the listless animals to the kennel.
Jack walked the black calf. Cal liked to see the livestock.
I overlooked the stockholder's lack of knowledge and skills.

16. c/d   accord broadcast calendar cold concluded could decade deduct
doctor education faces guidance handicapped indicate located
merchandise neglected occupied priced reduce second tendency

The educators could reach a decision before the proceedings.
He recommends an orthopedic doctor for my handicapped child.
Current records indicate a reduction in postcard production.

17. *u/y*   annually buying carefully duty equity fully guy hurry injury
laundry mutually naturally occupy poultry quantity regularly
summary truly unity usually utility voluntary you young your

You'll eventually qualify for jury duty. Study the summary.
Our community youngsters are studying the university survey.
Surgery is unnecessary for you. He is buying the gymnasium.

18. *f/d*   afford confuse defects defer drafts faced feeds fields finds
forced forward found friend fund identify justified notified
manufactured offered preferred qualified satisfied wonderful

The food was refrigerated. He was confused when confronted.
Federal funds financed our freedom. My fudge satisfied her.
Frieda's defendant was forced to testify in his own defense.

19. *c/v*   actively civic civil convert convey convince covers creative
curve device evidence invoice livestock objective productive
recovery services vacancy vacation vice vocational whichever

Vicky convinced the detectives that the devices were stolen.
The civilian serviced a blue convertible and other vehicles.
Victor has a clever plan to get an attractive vacation spot.

20. *g/h*   although bought bright caught delight enough fight gathering
growth bang hedge height higher huge interchange light might
night oversight paragraph right sight taught unchanged weigh

She bought four mahogany night stands and eight photographs.
The growth along the hedge at the interchange was very high.
Together we can do almost anything. The challenge is great.

21. *y/t*   ability beauty city duty empty fifty greatly hearty identity
jointly liberty mighty ninety pretty quietly royalty shortly
theory they tiny toys tray typist unity variety warranty yet

Did they get the disability payment? I hope they're strong.
I need forty or fifty temporary typists to type manuscripts.
Yvette and Roy should study for the yearly employment tests.

22. *s/w*   allowances bylaws crews drawings flowers highways interviews
knows laws news owns powers reviews saw sweet swing switches
towns wages was ways west whose wise wish words works writes

Six highway workers and one warehouse worker went on strike.
Bess writes that the wages in the western townships are low.
The newspaper review was shown to the two editors and staff.

23. d/k   backed breakdown dark desk drink kid kind kinds liked looked
worked weekend walked undertaking undertaken talked packaged
overlooked marked mankind knowledge kindly kindest undertake

Kit's dentist acknowledged that the desk was still unpacked.
Dick had a short weekend away from his desk. I worked late.
Kyle and Dirk overlooked the unmarked package. I like Dirk.

24. f/r   after breakfast colorful different enforce fairly far farmer
fire for form free fresh friend from grateful herself inform
manufacture nonprofit offers perfect reflect surface traffic

In the future, our factory will make every effort to comply.
I manufactured fourteen frames for their aircraft factories.
Rex favors a fast food franchise rather than a funeral home.

25. p/o   adopt bookkeeping copy deposit export follow-up groups hoping
import loop microphone nonpayment opens option output people
point policy pool port post report stop top upon valor pound

The supervisor called the prospective stenographers at home.
Did your group incorporate? I decided to employ a promoter.
Our team received cooperation in preparing a complex report.

26. r/u   accuracy brush church drugs enclosure feature graduate hours
incurred jury lumber measure nurse ours pure round rugs rule
run rural rush secured true under urge versus warehouse your

Unfortunately, the university trustee did not agree with us.
We figured that the citrus fruit would be seriously damaged.
Susan returned the resolution because it needed a signature.

27. s/e   assets business courses does estate eyes fresh guides houses
issues jobbers keeps less moves nose owners prices questions
rise seat see services set trees uses rates worse youngsters

Will the bankers allow the builders to construct apartments?
The candidates for the job of commissioner are all veterans.
I received several recommendations on the proposed policies.

28. g/t   argument budget cottage druggist eight forget gate get gifts
great hunting inviting judgment locating mighty nights ought
postage right strong tags things taught urgent voting weight

My suggestion was helpful in enabling Ted to find a cottage.
Forget my argument about the budget. Open the cottage gate.
The postage weight is right. Mark the flight tags "urgent."

29. *e/t*   attend bulletin create date extend estate erect enter forget
gate hotel item jet kept latest meter often plate quiet rate
site team teeth ten the tie ultimate united variety went yet.

Did we forget to extend the dates for the health conference?
The latest jet motor is extremely quiet. Will they buy one?
Their amateur team was ranked tenth in the statewide league.

30. *z/a*   analyzed authorization emphasize familiarize grazing hazards
jazz magazine organization personalized realized specialized
organize realizing stabilization standardization utilization

Zack realized that it's difficult to zigzag on a bike trail.
Did Sue realize that there is a new jazz magazine available?
The following begin with the letter z: zeal, zebra, zenana.

31. *s/c*   access because calls cans cars causes cents comes costs cuts
discuss economics fiscal historical inches justice mechanics
notices offices plastics respect scale scene schools tickets

Most schools sell tickets at the gate. Chris went to class.
Jo's college has had considerable success with scholarships.
Is it customary for our merchants to purchase their tickets?

32. *x/c/s*   exceeds exceptions excessive existence exclusive experiences
executives exchanges excerpts excels extracts excess excepts
excise excuse exercise excludes excursion exclusion lexicons

Rax's executives exercised extreme caution in the exchanges.
Roxy extracted excerpts from Sassoon's exclusive portfolios.
Rex has no excuse. He needs his exercise. Call Max's club.

33. *b/n*   abandoned band banks been behind beyond billing bonus branch
brings brown cabinets describing enabling handbook inability
lubrication nobody obtain plumbing ribbons subdivision urban

Are you describing my brown handbook? Ted brings bulletins.
A number of brand-new buildings were built by their brother.
The neighborhood bowling teams attended the benefit banquet.

34. *g/b*   agreeable bag banking bargain begin being big bigger billing
bridges brings brought budget buying contributing describing
establishing neighborhood obligations publishing subscribing

I asked Barb to get several large bags to hold their badges.
Gregg was describing the bowling tournament to Ben and Bert.
Gregory Gibbson is buying a big building for a banking firm.

35. i/k   asking backing checking drinking ink kid kind king kit knife
knowing liked marketing mild parking packaging quickly risks
skilled speaking strike talking thinking undertaking walking

Kim is checking the bookkeeping. Did Mike notice a mistake?
Dick is skilled in keeping livestock. Mike is going skiing.
We think it is a mistake to take such a risk. Do you agree?

36. q/a   acquainted adequately banquet equals equivalent headquarters
inadequate liquidate qualified quantities quart quota square
equal quarts quarters qualification quotations questionnaire

Dominique drove Abigail to the quarterfinals in Albuquerque.
My quarterback quickly passed to Quincy late in the quarter.
Monique mailed two questionnaires to Chiquita in Quincy, MA.

37. t/f   after benefit conflict draft effort fact faith fast feet fit
flat football gift hereafter itself manufacture notify often
platform reflects shaft theft thoughtful traffic unfortunate

The footballs were a gift from my staff to the team members.
The traffic jam caused Betty to walk to her downtown office.
The temperature for the game was fifty. Angie was grateful.

38. s/k   asks backs clerk desks folks inks keys kits likewise markets
parks risk seek sick skiing sky speak stake stock takes task
tanks skin textbooks thanks tickets tracks weeks workmanship

After breakfast we went skiing. Kristy needed six blankets.
Kelvin suggested we use textbooks in our knitting workshops.
The packages were lost with the keys. Kelly made a mistake.

Progressive Practice

The next two sets of drills—alphabetic and numeric—provide material for 20-second, 30-second, and 1-minute timings. Use these drills to develop speed, to determine at what speed you key most accurately, and to help you develop the habit of watching the copy, not the keyboard.

Speed Building

To increase your speed, follow these steps:

1. Determine the line that you can barely complete in the time allowed.
2. Ask someone to time you, calling "Return!" at the end of the time allowed.
3. When "Return!" is called, press the [Enter] key.
   a. If you finished the sentence, begin the next one.
   b. If you did not finish the sentence, repeat it.

4. Take a rest break after five or six timed trials.

Switch to working on accuracy only after you have improved your speed four to six wpm—and vice versa.

For example, if you are using 20-second timings and are keying at 24 wpm, begin working for speed on sentence 11. Once you have reached 30 wpm (sentence 15), drop back to 27 wpm (sentence 13) and work for accuracy. Switch back to speed development once you have reached 30 wpm (sentence 15).

Accuracy Development

To increase your accuracy, follow these steps:

1. Repeat steps 1 and 2 in the "Speed Building" section, after asking the timer to call "Stop!" at the end of the time allowed.

2. Take approximately ten seconds to proofread your work.
   a. If you did not finish the sentence, repeat the sentence on the next trial.
   b. If you finished the sentence but made more than one error, repeat the sentence on the next trial.
   c. If you finished the sentence and had no errors or only one error, go on to the next sentence for the next trial.

3. Repeat the process.

Progressive Practice—Alphabetic Series

Keyboard the lines, following the instructions in the "Speed Building" and "Accuracy Development" sections. Use word wrap. At the end of each day, record on the Progressive Practice Charts where you stopped.

WPM in				
20"	30"	1'		
9	6	3	**1.**	Copy this note.
	7		**2.**	Have a good time.
12	8	4	**3.**	I wish I could swim.
	9		**4.**	One of my cars is old.
15	10	5	**5.**	The checks are not ready.
	11		**6.**	Remember to read your book.
18	12	6	**7.**	Do not forget your assignment.
	13		**8.**	I thought the order was missing.
21	14	7	**9.**	Make a shopping list for all items.
	15		**10.**	Always use a budget to make ends meet.
24	16	8	**11.**	Practice being an alert, aware consumer.
	17		**12.**	Please take the messages to their offices.

27 18 9   **13.** Constantly scan the ads and get the bargains.

19   **14.** Compare labels on items to get your best values.

30 20 10   **15.** Resist buying goods you cannot afford; buy wisely.

33 22 11   **16.** It is important for you to know how to handle conflict.

36 24 12   **17.** As an alert shopper, demand your rights in the marketplace.

39 26 13   **18.** After a discussion, my lawyers drew up a legal agreement to sign.

42 28 14   **19.** If I were the one arranging for tours, I would prepare three booklets.

45 30 15   **20.** If you know who lost a leather briefcase, please contact us at this office.

48 32 16   **21.** We have been asked to give an address at the next meeting of the branch chapter.

51 34 17   **22.** Please let me know as soon as possible whether you can be of assistance to our group.

54 36 18   **23.** My questions to you are quite simple. Most of them involve collecting data for my speech.

57 38 19   **24.** I am sure you could prepare a rough draft of my speech. Can it be finished by my next meeting?

60 40 20   **25.** The general theme of this convention will be consumerism. Bob expects a large number to register.

42 21   **26.** The staff tried their hardest to meet deadlines, since quick action was an important objective for us all.

44 22   **27.** New assignments were given to everyone who was attending the meeting. Confidential files were also delivered.

46 23   **28.** When I opened her file, the computerized report was missing. I quickly called her office, but she had already left.

48 24   **29.** The customer thought he had ordered one copy of the booklet. However, he discovered that four copies had been delivered.

50 25   **30.** The local warehouse notified our boss that there would be a long delay in filling the order for consumer pamphlets and books.

52 26   **31.** We felt that the cost of textbooks would increase by August. In May, we were surprised to learn that the cost had not yet changed.

27   **32.** Our supervisor, Jo Miller, decided to adopt flexible office hours for the computer staff. The staff was delighted with her new policy.

28   **33.** Any shopper may be confused by the endless array of brand names, packages, and special sale promotions to be found in most grocery stores.

29 **34.** Our manager informed the merchant that the goods would not be shipped until we received a check to cover the cost of the goods we sent in August.

30 **35.** There is usually a difference of opinion between a referee and a coach on procedural calls. However, the referee has the final authority in disputes.

31 **36.** Selecting foods with nutrient content in mind will help you improve and maintain the quality of your diet. Read the labels to identify the many nutrients.

32 **37.** One of the advantages of renting is that most needed repairs are taken care of by the landlord. Your rent pays, at least partly, for this valuable convenience.

33 **38.** Plan early on a career. As the economy grows and as new technologies and ways of doing business are developed, the choice of careers from which to choose increases.

34 **39.** We need to learn how to be good consumers. We need to learn how to get exactly what we need at a good price without much difficulty. This is what makes a good consumer.

35 **40.** Good consumers are those who know how to obtain information about the products or services they are buying and are able to make reasonable decisions based on that information.

36 **41.** Cars, newspapers, radios, bathtubs, guided missiles, eating utensils, books, and pencil sharpeners all have at least one thing in common. They are made by workers in our factories.

37 **42.** We should know about the concept of product liability. The government has established a commission to help us. The commission makes rules as to safety standards for consumer products.

38 **43.** Computers can process large quantities of data rapidly and correctly but only if they are given specific instructions to follow. Computer programmers must write these detailed instructions.

39 **44.** It's generally accepted that there are seven elements that contribute to effective written communication: conciseness, completeness, courtesy, attractiveness, accuracy, clarity, and simplicity.

40 **45.** Finding enjoyable and suitable work is not a simple matter. Many individuals discover their liking or disliking for particular kinds of jobs only after they have been working for weeks or even months.

41 **46.** Any formula that will help you to choose wisely, therefore, is most essential. Schooling, hobbies, personality traits, interests, ability, energy, and health all enter into your own job selection process.

42 **47.** The higher you plan to climb up the employment ladder, the more thoroughly you must plan your preparation. There are career opportunities in many fields. However, competition is keen and you must be prepared.

43 **48.** The laws of supply and demand have a great influence on both securing and keeping a job. If the supply of workers with specialized training is less than the demand, then you can be more selective in choosing a job.

44 **49.** While business reserves the right to select the person most suited to its needs, it is up to you to accept the job you desire. The skills and knowledge you acquire will be useful commodities when you apply for your job.

45 **50.** A career that will be continually challenging is not that easy to find. That is why you owe it to yourself to take a good look at several industries that are dynamic and in need of imaginative people. Can you qualify today?

46 **51.** Success in any business is founded on cooperation. Unless we practice it, there is a lack of unity and purpose and the results can be disastrous. It is often the little warm and friendly considerations that make the most impact.

47 **52.** Walking is free--it does not require any expensive equipment or fancy clothing. It does not require advanced planning, reservations, or perfect weather. It can be done alone or in groups. A brisk walk is invigorating. Try it today.

48 **53.** Communication is defined as an exchange of information and ideas. This exchange may be oral or written. The origin of oral communication is as old as history itself. Today, much of the communication that takes place in the world is oral.

49 **54.** Oral communications form the basis of many human activities. Business and industry are using television, telephone, and radio for more and better communications. Today, we have many different forms of oral media that are available to business.

50 **55.** In nearly everything in which we participate, there is some good and some bad. Some aspects of a job will be appealing to some workers and not to others and vice versa. Thus, give and take is a requisite to effective relations in the world of work.

Progressive Practice—Numeric and Symbols Series

Keyboard these lines, following the instructions in the "Speed Building" and "Accuracy Development" sections, found earlier in this lesson. Use word wrap. At the end of each day, use the Progressive Practice Charts at the end of this lesson to record where you stopped. Your performance on these sentences will differ significantly from that on the alphabetic sentences.

WPM in		
20"	30"	1'

18 12 6   **1.** EZ Co. reported a loss of 10%.

21 14 7   **2.** "Who's calling?" asked Karen Goetz.

24 16 8   **3.** The book was called "How to Typewrite."

27 18 9   **4.** Is Rummel & Jay located at 19450 High Street?

30 20 10   **5.** I said that three months (13 weeks) make a quarter.

33 22 11   **6.** Send the 11 manuscripts c/o A. Olinzock, Apartment #54.

36 24 12   **7.** Helen said, "Do you think it's time to plan for my holiday?"

39 26 13   **8.** All first-class mail is to be deposited by 9:30 a.m. Don't wait.

42 28 14   **9.** Max's pencils sell for 20 cents. I paid $3.50 for a dozen #2 pencils!

45 30 15   **10.** Plan on using an asterisk (*) for footnotes. Type the * after a reference.*

48 32 16   **11.** Janice was asked to type addresses on #10 envelopes. It may take her two hours.

51 34 17   **12.** Use the diagonal(/) as follows: bacon and/or eggs; OS/as; 5/9; 237/620; w/o wheels.

54 36 18   **13.** You may use the symbol (#) in technical writing. The serial number of the part is #30112.

57 38 19   **14.** Note the following uses of the (!): Terrific! Hurry! Get that! Fantastic! Worry! Oh! No!

60 40 20   **15.** I opened the second-class mail at 8:30 a.m. The letter said that the conference would be June 9-18.

42 21   **16.** She asked if a temperature of 99 and humidity of 87% would make a difference in the game's starting time.

44 22   **17.** The tax started at 1% in 1945. It became 3% in 1952. Next, it was 4%. Now it's up to 6%. I expect 1% more.

46 23   **18.** Bass & Co. announced a sale of all "ready to wear" items for the week of May 9-15. Sophia bought a size 12 blouse.

48 24   **19.** The interest rate fluctuated between 18% and 19% this past year. I expect to see an interest rate of 20% by September.

50 25   **20.** The Bureau's model contained projections of gross national product (GNP). Detailed information is given in BL Bulletin 2030.

52 26   **21.** Between 1978 and 1990, employment in the service industries was expected to increase from 16 to 24.4 million workers or 53 percent.

27 **22.** Accounting Clerks (D.O.T. 216.482-010), sometimes known as bookkeeping clerks, perform a variety of tasks. Pete can list most of them.

28 **23.** A detailed description of Model X1781 appears in Bulletin 18. Model X1781 was developed by the Department of Commerce on November 26, 1964.

29 **24.** Please send us the following: 12 gallons of paint #D3067 @ $9.50; 18 gallons of thinner #158B @ $5.95; and 10 gallons of paint #304C210 @ $8.50.

30 **25.** I can save 30 cents on each 2-liter bottle of soda if I buy it by June 19. If I buy 4 bottles @ 89 cents each, I will have saved $1.20. Can I have the $15.50?

31 **26.** The following ad caught my eye: Kentucky Cooking! Pumpkin/zucchini bread (3 recipes in one) and chocolate Derby pie! 95 cents, SASE, PO Box 164, Willows, KY.

32 **27.** The book by Hiscott and Nice* contained the following math equations: 154 + 200 = 354; 52 + 10 = 62; 40/2 = 20; 10 * 5 = 50. Jenning's assistant helped us prove them.

33 **28.** Between 1978 and 1990, wholesale and retail trade employment was expected to grow from 19.4 to 24.8 million workers. This is about a 28.1 percent increase (Chart 6).

34 **29.** The 45-minute film "A Day at the Stock Exchange" will be available on June 17. I have another film, "Managing Your Money" (in color), that will be available next week.

35 **30.** Our economist wanted to use an asterisk (*) as a reference for her tables. She referenced them as follows: Table 1*, Table 2**, Table 3***. I suggested using another style.

36 **31.** They copied the following responses from the opinion survey: "Definitely, 23"; "Probably, 14"; "Possibly, 46"; and "Yes, 84." They need to find out the percent of "Yes" responses.

37 **32.** The classified ad read as follows: VCR BUYER'S COMPARISON-- Latest brands/models $3.50 or self-addressed envelope for details. Video Values (VR), 39 Shore Pky #3D, Columbus, OH 43210.

38 **33.** The computer printout showed the following data: 6/17/81; order number OS269/32/3618; 175 cases of #6 3/4 envelopes; order number OS358/21/2528; 12 cases of #10 envelopes; ship by 11/26/81.

39 **34.** Jan found that, in 1974, single-element typewriters outsold typebar electrics 520,000 to 430,000; in 1975, 600,000 to 390,000; and by 1976, 745,000 to 350,000, or by a margin of more than 2 to 1.

40 **35.** The price for the publication was $10 for the single volume; $2 each for the separate booklets; and $12 for the packaged set of 9 booklets. A brochure listing the chapter titles is shown on page 661.

ALPHABETIC 20"

Date	Beginning Sentence Number	S/A*	Last Sentence Number Completed	S/A*
9/30	13	S	15	S
9/31	13	A		

FIGURE 27.1

An example of a completed Progressive Practice Chart.

Using Progressive Practice Charts

To record your progress in the Progressive Practice Charts, refer to Figure 27.1 and follow these steps:

1. Determine the timing you will be using—for example, 20".

2. Locate the corresponding chart in the Progressive Practice Charts. (See Figures 27.2, 27.3, 27.4, 27.5, 27.6, and 27.7.)

3. Enter today's date.

4. Enter the number of the sentence on which you will begin keying. Note your objective: S=Speed, A=Accuracy.

5. When you have completed a drill, or when you want to move from one objective to the other, record the number of the sentence you last completed, along with the objective—for example, 15S.

ALPHABETIC 20"

Date	Beginning Sentence Number	S/A*	Last Sentence Number Completed	S/A*

*S = Speed Goal; A = Accuracy Goal

FIGURE 27.2

Alphabetic 20" Progressive Practice Chart.

ALPHABETIC 30"

Date	Beginning Sentence Number	S/A*	Last Sentence Number Completed	S/A*

*S = Speed Goal; A = Accuracy Goal

FIGURE 27.3
*Alphabetic 30"
Progressive Practice
Chart.*

ALPHABETIC 1'

Date	Beginning Sentence Number	S/A*	Last Sentence Number Completed	S/A*

*S = Speed Goal; A = Accuracy Goal

FIGURE 27.4
*Alphabetic 1'
Progressive Practice
Chart.*

NUMERIC 20"

FIGURE 27.5

*Numeric 20"
Progressive Practice
Chart.*

Date	Beginning Sentence Number	S/A*	Last Sentence Number Completed	S/A*

*S = Speed Goal; A = Accuracy Goal

NUMERIC 30"

FIGURE 27.6

*Numeric 30"
Progressive Practice
Chart.*

Date	Beginning Sentence Number	S/A*	Last Sentence Number Completed	S/A*

*S = Speed Goal; A = Accuracy Goal

NUMERIC 1'

FIGURE 27.7
*Numeric 1'
Progressive Practice
Chart.*

Date	Beginning Sentence Number	S/A*	Last Sentence Number Completed	S/A*

*S = Speed Goal; A = Accuracy Goal

6. If you move to another objective, record the sentence number and objective on the next line—for example, 13A.

Lesson 28   Straight-Copy Timings

All the straight-copy timings should be double-spaced for ease in proofreading. Use word wrap. When you have completed a page of text, WordPerfect 5.1 automatically inserts a line of dashes (-) across the screen to show that you are working on a new page.

If you keyboard all of the copy before the allotted time has elapsed, start over. Each timing is marked for one-, three-, and five-minute timings. The one-minute timings vary from 41 to 99 wpm. Two hyphens (--) indicate that that line should *not* be used for a one-minute timing.

Difficulty of Timings

The timings in this lesson have been analyzed for stroke difficulty and are generally of average difficulty when compared with the difficulty of "real-world" business communications. All the timings are approximately the same level of difficulty so that you can easily measure your progress.

Determining Keyboarding Speed

To determine your keyboarding speed, follow these steps:

1. Find the speed in the appropriate column to the right for the last *full* line keyboarded.
2. Add to that figure the partial-line credit from the scale at the bottom of the timing.

   EXAMPLE: In a five-minute timing of "Report Writing," a student completes the word **projects** in line two of the fifth paragraph. From the GWPM (5') column, the speed to the end of the last complete line is 42. The last word keyboarded appears above the 2 in the 5' scale at the bottom of the page. The total gross words per minute (GWPM) is 44 (42 + 2).

Recording Speed and Accuracy Scores

To see how your performance, speed, and accuracy have improved over time, you may want to record your scores regularly on the Performance Graph shown in Figure 28.1.

To use the graphs follow these steps (see Figure 28.2 for an example of a completed graph):

1. In the **speed** column, put a number in front of the bottom **0** to create a number below which you know your speed will not fall— for example, 20.
2. Record the month and date at the top of the next blank column.
3. Record the length of the timing at the very bottom of the blank column.
4. Place an **S** on the graph in the blank column opposite the GWPM speed obtained on the timing.
5. Place an **E** on the graph in the same column opposite the number of errors obtained on the timing.
6. To make the graph, join the S's from column to column; do the same with the E's.

   Don't worry if your accuracy score fluctuates greatly—accuracy is not a reliable measure. Speed scores, however, should be more consistent, since speed is a highly reliable measure.

FIGURE 28.1 *A Performance Graph is used to chart your progress.*

PERFORMANCE GRAPH

Name _____   Class _____

Month: __:__

Date: __:__

Errors	Speed
49	9
48	8
47	7
46	6
45	5
44	4
43	3
42	2
41	1
40	0
39	9
38	8
37	7
36	6
35	5
34	4
33	3
32	2
31	1
30	0
29	9
28	8
27	7
26	6
25	5
24	4
23	3
22	2
21	1
20	0
19	9
18	8
17	7
16	6
15	5
14	4
13	3
12	2
11	1
10	0
9	9
8	8
7	7
6	6
5	5
4	4
3	3
2	2
1	1
0	0

Length of
Timing (in') __:__

FIGURE 28.2 *An example of a completed Performance Graph.*

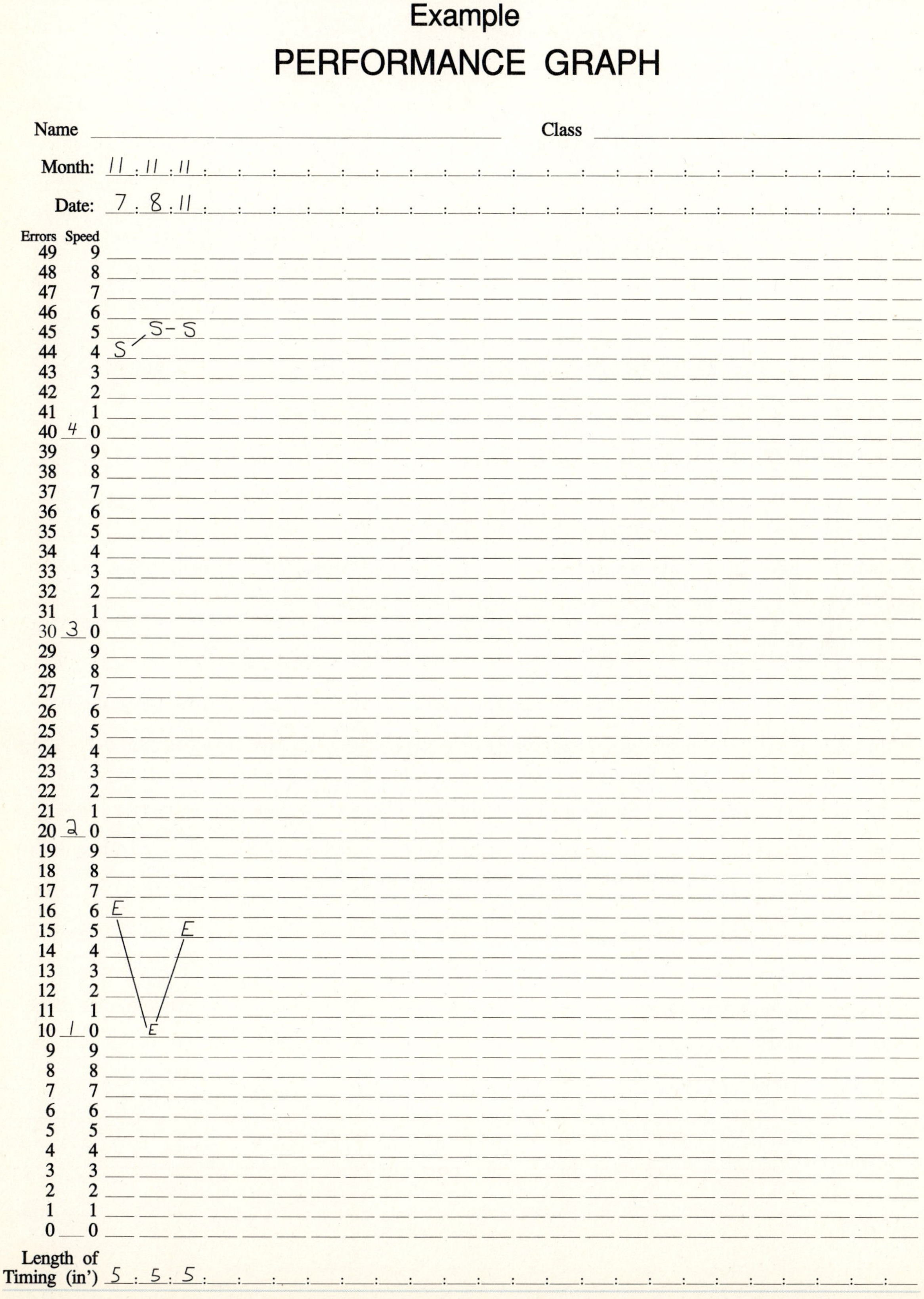

Example
PERFORMANCE GRAPH

Name _____   Class _____

Month: _11_ ; _11_ ; _11_ ; ___ ; ___ ; ___ ; ___ ; ___ ; ___ ; ___ ; ___ ; ___ ; ___ ; ___ ; ___ ; ___ ; ___ ; ___ ;

Date: _7_ ; _8_ ; _11_ ; ___ ; ___ ; ___ ; ___ ; ___ ; ___ ; ___ ; ___ ; ___ ; ___ ; ___ ; ___ ; ___ ; ___ ; ___ ;

Errors	Speed	
49	9	
48	8	
47	7	
46	6	
45	5	S–S
44	4	S
43	3	
42	2	
41	1	
40 4	0	
39	9	
38	8	
37	7	
36	6	
35	5	
34	4	
33	3	
32	2	
31	1	
30 3	0	
29	9	
28	8	
27	7	
26	6	
25	5	
24	4	
23	3	
22	2	
21	1	
20 2	0	
19	9	
18	8	
17	7	
16	6	E
15	5	E
14	4	
13	3	
12	2	
11	1	
10 1	0	E
9	9	
8	8	
7	7	
6	6	
5	5	
4	4	
3	3	
2	2	
1	1	
0	0	

Length of
Timing (in') _5_ ; _5_ ; _5_ ; ___ ; ___ ; ___ ; ___ ; ___ ; ___ ; ___ ; ___ ; ___ ; ___ ; ___ ; ___ ; ___ ; ___ ;

Timing #1   **Report Writing**

13	4	3	Writing a report need not be the ordeal so many of us fear
26	9	5	it to be and sometimes find it to be. Like so many other things,
40	13	8	it is not quite so difficult if we break it down into small jobs.
53	18	11	The purpose of the timed writings in this text is to explain how
66	22	13	to write a report in a systematic way. While all the suggestions
80	27	16	will not be necessary for every report, the principles presented
83	28	17	will be generally useful.

13	32	19	Reports should be written constructively. Instead of
25	36	22	repeating cliches or plodding through an account of some meeting
36	40	24	or convention, it is much more interesting to offer exciting,
45	43	26	thought-provoking interpretations and ideas.

12	47	28	To prepare a good report, you need to be dependable,
25	51	31	patient, and resourceful, as well as hard-working. This is the
37	55	33	recipe for holding the interest of listeners and readers. It is
48	59	35	the only way to convey to others the results of research.

--	66	39	There are basically two kinds of business reports: the
--	63	38	information report and the research report.

12	70	42	The information report is to keep an executive up-to-date
25	74	44	with events, developments, and projects. The research report is
37	78	47	the outcome of your investigation of a specific topic of
49	82	49	interest. This might include any area of human activity, from
61	86	52	politics to labor relations, from an idea about recycling energy
72	90	54	to discovering new ways of using available energy.

12	94	56	Any report upon which action may be based, or which may
25	98	59	influence executives in one direction or another, is an important
37	102	61	piece of work and deserves our utmost attention. There are few
49	106	64	more interesting jobs than that of searching for material to be
55	108	65	used in such a report.

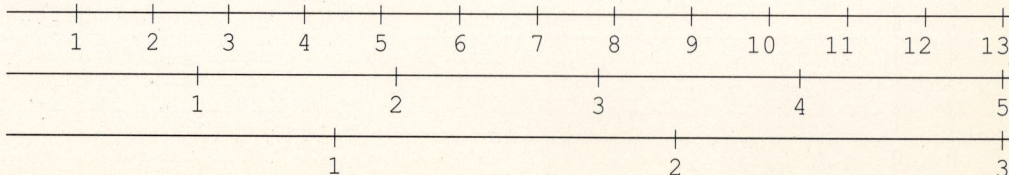

1 2 3 4 5 6 7 8 9 10 11 12 13

1 2 3 4 5

1 2 3

Preparing to Write a Report

Timing #2

12	4	2	The work of writing a report begins long before you make a
24	8	5	move for a pen or toward the keyboard. You must understand
36	12	7	exactly what is wanted and why it is wanted. The report must
49	16	10	address definite and limited problems. The responsibility for
62	21	12	acquiring a proper background for writing the report is a joint
75	25	15	one shared by each writer and the person requesting the report.

12	29	17	The following steps, if followed in order, should be very
24	33	20	helpful in preparing any report: understand what you are
37	37	22	required to write; determine all possible sources of information;
50	42	25	decide which sources are available to you as well as which ones
62	46	27	you wish to use; gather the information along with any
74	50	30	explanations needed; sort the evidence; bring all of the
87	54	32	available evidence together; pull out what is useful for the
--	58	35	report and discard the rest; organize the remaining information
--	61	36	into report form; and then summarize your findings.

12	65	39	There are at least four limits placed on the research that
24	69	41	can be undertaken: time, staff, money, and data. It is
36	73	44	important for the report writer to do the best job possible
48	77	46	within these limits. It is also important for the writer to
60	81	48	state clearly any weaknesses in the report because of these
72	85	51	limitations. When reference is made to the report in future
84	89	53	years, the reader will want to know the sources used and the
96	93	56	difficulties encountered. This knowledge will assist future
109	97	58	researchers in updating or following up on the research report.
--	101	61	In addition, the reader of the report will not be misled into
--	105	63	drawing faulty conclusions because of a lack of information.

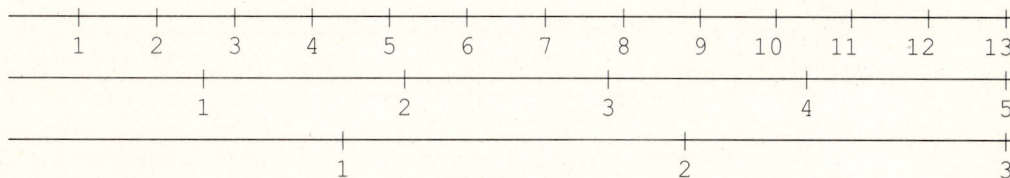

```
  |    |    |    |    |    |    |    |    |    |    |    |    |
  1    2    3    4    5    6    7    8    9   10   11   12   13
     |         |         |         |         |         |
     1         2         3         4         5
          |                   |                   |
          1                   2                   3
```

Timing #3   **The Objective of a Report**

13	4	3	In planning any report, serious thought needs to be given to
25	8	5	the reasons why the report was requested in the first place and
37	12	7	the personality and expectations of the person for whom the
50	17	10	report is to be prepared. Some people want great detail, while
63	21	13	others will be content with conclusions; some will want tables
76	25	15	and graphs, while others will find statistics boring and perhaps
82	27	16	too difficult to understand.
13	32	19	A report that is designed to provide information on which an
25	36	21	executive can make a decision is helpful. It helps determine
38	40	24	what is right and what is wrong in the business, and it gives an
50	44	26	interpretation to guide the business to a solution if one is
52	45	27	needed.
12	49	29	The objective for some reports is simply to report the
25	53	32	evidence located. For other reports the recommendations made on
38	57	34	the evidence gathered become the most important objectives of the
50	61	37	reports. There are two occasions when recommendations by the
63	66	39	report writer are usually in order: when they are specifically
75	70	42	requested and when the report writer believes that there is
87	74	44	something to be recommended, based on his or her knowledge,
93	76	45	experience, and other qualities.
12	80	48	When recommendations are made, they should be based on the
25	84	50	evidence presented within the body of the report. They should be
37	88	53	clear and definite. They should tell what to do, who is to do
49	92	55	it, where it should be done, at what time, why this is
62	96	58	recommended, and, if possible, the costs associated with the
65	97	58	actions suggested.

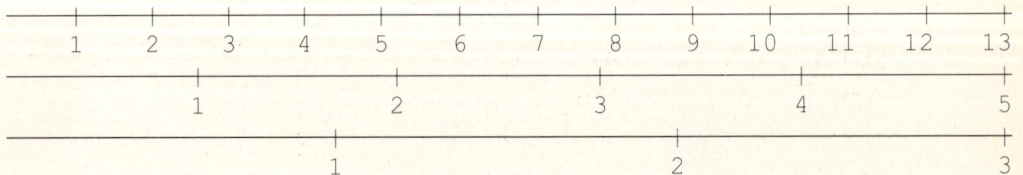

Timing #4

The Form of a Report

12	4	2	Writing a report, unless it is very short, is usually much
24	8	5	easier if an outline is prepared first. For an inexperienced
37	12	7	report writer, the first step might be to write one sentence in
50	17	10	which the objective of the study is established. This will help
63	21	13	the writer focus attention on the primary purpose of the report.
75	25	15	This statement might then be followed with main headings and
88	29	18	subheadings growing out of the main purpose statement and moving
95	32	19	toward the report's conclusions.

13	36	22	Following this approach will help eliminate vague direction,
25	40	24	fill gaps in information and reasoning, and keep the writer
38	44	27	focused. The outline will also help the writer keep in mind the
50	48	29	needs of the readers by providing a logical, step-by-step
54	50	30	organization to the report.

12	54	32	Although it does not hold true in every situation, the
24	58	30	success of many reports may be attributed to a well-written
37	62	37	introduction. If the reader's attention can be gained right from
50	66	40	the beginning, the chances are much greater that the body of the
62	70	42	report will be read with the kind of attention desired by the
63	71	42	writer.

13	75	45	Beyond the outline and the introductory section, there are
25	79	47	many other parts to a good report. If the report is lengthy,
37	83	50	there may be a title page, a table of contents, an index,
50	87	52	appendices, reference lists, footnotes, and so on. Regardless of
63	92	55	length, however, most reports will mention the procedures used to
76	96	58	obtain the evidence in the report, and the evidence itself. When
89	100	60	needed, conclusions and recommendations appear at the end of the
--	105	63	report. Because there are so many styles and forms used for
--	108	65	typing reports, such details are not given here.

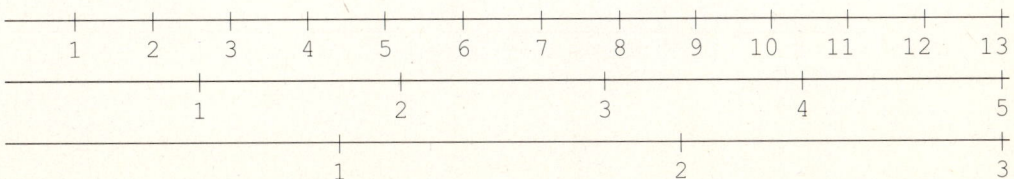

```
    |   |   |   |   |   |   |   |   |   |   |   |   |
    1   2   3   4   5   6   7   8   9  10  11  12  13
        |       |       |       |       |
        1       2       3       4       5
            |           |           |
            1           2           3
```

Timing #5   **Types of Business Reports (1)**

12	4	2	Selection of the most appropriate type of research is a
24	8	5	critical factor in the success of the final report with its
30	10	6	conclusions and recommendations.

13	14	9	The person who writes a report that records happenings in
25	18	11	the order of their time sequence is involved in writing a
38	24	14	chronological report. It is important in writing such a report
50	27	16	to keep in mind that events sometimes follow one another in
63	31	19	successive points of time without moving toward a common end.
75	35	21	There may often be a temptation to find cause-and-effect
88	39	24	relationships where no evidence exists for such a conclusion.
--	43	26	The report should be limited to facts without assuming a
--	47	28	relationship among the facts. Such research should indicate
--	52	31	origin, history, and development. To be effective, however, such
--	56	34	research must include the asking of important questions and the
--	60	36	posing of potential answers. Otherwise, the report becomes only
--	62	37	a collection of isolated facts.

13	66	40	The analytical report starts off with the idea that there is
26	70	42	a problem to be solved and moves toward definite conclusions. It
39	75	45	is not merely a collection of ideas or data; it gathers facts for
52	79	47	and against the proposal being studied and then goes on to assess
64	83	50	them by comparison and testing. The writer of such a report
77	87	52	needs to have an open mind. The objective is to find as much of
90	92	55	the truth, in a clear and unbiased way, as possible. Looking for
--	96	58	new insight along the way may require a shift in direction. A
--	100	60	good writer is willing to follow the path opened up by the new
--	100	60	facts.

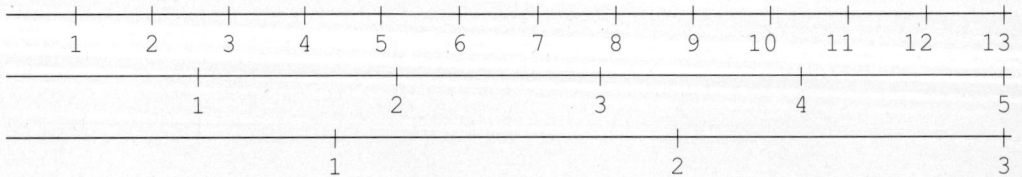

```
      1    2    3    4    5    6    7    8    9   10   11   12   13
           1         2         3         4              5
                1              2              3
```

Timing #6   **Types of Business Reports (2)**

13	4	3	The bulk of business report writing is designed to answer
25	8	5	these questions: What is true? What is best? What is
38	13	8	necessary? How do we do it? A final question to be asked when
51	17	10	the others have been answered is: If I do that, then what will
64	21	13	happen? A good way to check out how successfully the report has
77	26	15	been completed is to compare the analysis with those of earlier
90	30	18	writers, to determine if an original focus has been developed, to
--	34	21	examine the alternative courses of action proposed along with the
--	38	23	probable consequences of each, and to judge whether the report
--	40	24	clearly states what was intended.

12	44	26	There are other types of reports. A case study, which may
24	48	29	be incomplete in and of itself because of the difficulty of
37	52	31	drawing conclusions from only one case, may be useful as a part
49	56	34	of a larger project. Its major use may be to suggest problems
62	61	36	and solutions to explore in a larger study. Its major advantage
74	65	39	is that the problem can be explored thoroughly because of the
86	69	41	limited scope involved. Some genetic studies may trace the
99	73	44	development of their subjects, stressing the casual sequence of
--	77	46	events. A comparative study will involve bringing together all
--	79	47	of the important facts.

12	83	50	In summary, the greatest impact and best organization will
24	87	52	be gained when the report contains these components: the
37	91	55	objectives of the report, factors which affect whether or not the
50	95	57	objectives will be reached, the options open to the company and
63	100	60	to the competition, and the courses of action being recommended.

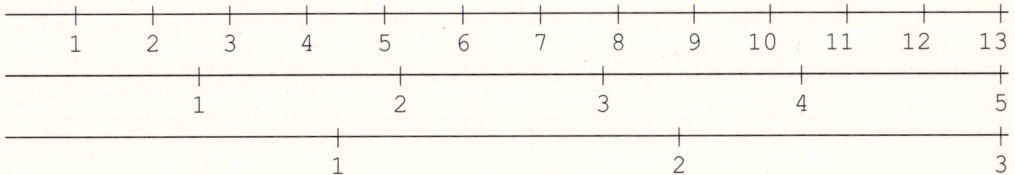

```
    +----+----+----+----+----+----+----+----+----+----+----+----+
       1    2    3    4    5    6    7    8    9   10   11   12   13
    +---------+---------+---------+---------+---------+
         1         2         3         4         5
    +--------------+--------------+--------------+
           1              2              3
```

Timing #7   **Sources of Information**

12	4	2	Collecting data is the basis of all good reports. This
24	8	5	advice was given by Edison: "The first thing is to find out
36	12	7	everything everybody else knows, and then begin where they left
37	12	7	off."

13	17	10	While all problems will have their own requirements, there
26	21	13	are sources of data that are common to nearly all: observations,
38	25	15	tests, books, surveys, interviews, accounting records, and the
50	29	17	records of meetings and workshops. The successful writer will
62	33	20	use data from any source that will help meet the goals of the
64	34	20	report.

13	38	23	Data may be primary or secondary. Just as in the law, the
26	42	25	word of an eyewitness is more valuable than that of a person who
39	47	28	testifies secondhand. In business and other reports, firsthand
52	51	31	data are to be preferred to other sources. Often, observations
65	55	33	can be checked against what other writers have concluded. Once
77	59	36	again it is important for the writer to have enough self-
90	64	38	confidence to be willing to take a stand somewhat different from
--	68	41	that of other writers. A person who echoes what others have
--	72	43	written, without careful review of that writing, will not be held
--	74	44	in high esteem by others.

13	78	47	Secondary sources are valued because of their accuracy. The
25	82	49	reasoning contained in these sources must be well thought out.
37	86	52	The case under study should match closely the case being
50	90	54	reported. No statement is more reliable than its source. The
63	95	57	report writer must spend long hours in gathering facts, arranging
76	99	59	them, interpreting them, and then as much time in rechecking the
81	101	60	accuracy of what is available.

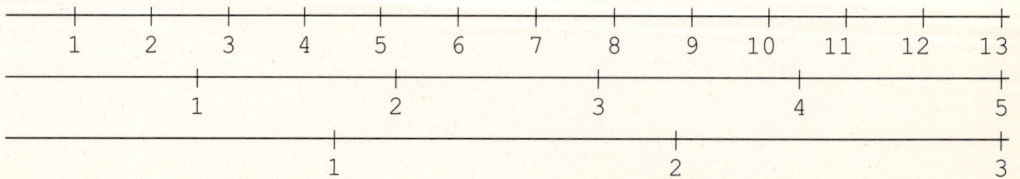

Writing the Report (1)

Timing #8

13	4	3	Having gathered the facts and organized them according to an
25	8	5	outline, the next step is to compose the report. Skill in the
38	13	8	art of writing is not acquired without considerable hard work and
50	17	10	practice. It takes discipline to set aside the time to
63	21	13	concentrate. It takes practice to express ideas in an exciting
76	25	15	and interesting way for the readers. It takes a willingness to
89	30	18	listen to the evaluation of others so that improvement can take
--	34	20	place. Finally, it takes conviction that accuracy and honesty
--	38	23	are desired so that a believable report can result. Beyond these
--	43	26	characteristics, however, there are ways in which a person can
--	47	28	improve writing skills. Some suggestions for doing this follow.
13	51	31	The report must be practical. Writers often fall into the
26	55	33	trap of writing what they think their audience wants to hear. Or
38	59	36	they make the mistake of using the report as a vehicle for
50	63	38	promoting their own ideas. If a writer is to have credibility,
63	68	41	then the information must be presented just as it was found, not
73	71	43	as the writer might have wanted to find the evidence.
13	75	45	The report must be complete. It is essential for the writer
26	80	48	to include all of the information that will help the reader reach
39	84	50	a decision related to the objectives of the report. This means
52	88	53	that both favorable and unfavorable facts will be included, along
65	93	56	with pros and cons for each option proposed. Any report that is
78	97	58	written with only one point of view is going to be biased and may
87	100	60	lead to incorrect and misleading conclusions.

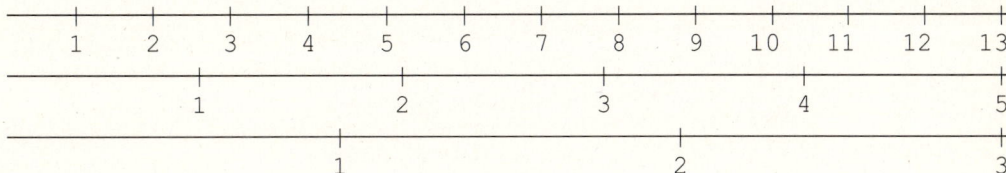

```
|---+---+---+---+---+---+---+---+---+---+---+---+---|
    1   2   3   4   5   6   7   8   9   10  11  12  13
|-----------+-----------+-----------+-----------+----|
            1           2           3           4    5
|-----------------+-----------------+-----------------|
                  1                 2                 3
```

Timing #9   **Writing the Report (2)**

13	4	3	The report must be clear. Only the careful organization of
25	8	5	facts and interpretation will enable readers to follow the
38	13	8	writer's reasoning. The art of good writing lies not so much in
50	17	10	how extensive the writer's vocabulary is as in how that
63	21	13	vocabulary is used. It consists of using the right word in the
75	25	15	right place to convey the right idea. If readers do not under-
88	29	18	stand what the writer is trying to accomplish, then the purpose
--	34	20	of the report has been missed. As Alice in Wonderland commented,
--	38	23	"Somehow it seems to fill my head with ideas--only I don't
--	39	24	exactly know what they are."

13	44	26	Another way in which clarity is missed is through the use of
25	48	29	trite expressions. Their use indicates that the writer has
38	52	31	little imagination or originality. The persons receiving the
51	56	34	report could well judge that such a writer had not analyzed the
63	60	36	problem well. Jargon, or words that have a special meaning to
76	65	39	one group, is acceptable, and perhaps even necessary, only when
89	69	41	it is known that everyone reading the report will understand its
--	73	44	meaning. When a report is written for a general audience, jargon
--	75	45	is definitely unacceptable.

12	79	47	The report must be honest. The facts presented must be
24	83	50	accurate. A clear distinction should be made between what is
36	87	52	opinion, what is assumed, and what is factual. Opinion and
48	91	54	assumptions should be clearly identified and not presented as
49	91	55	facts.

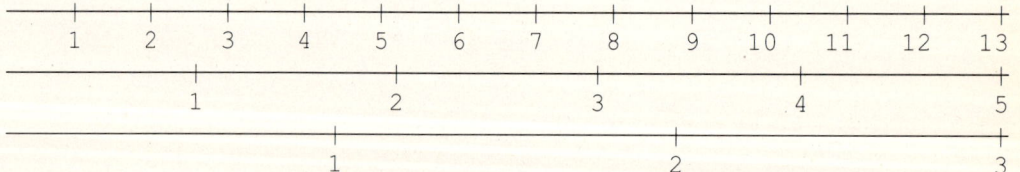

```
+---+---+---+---+---+---+---+---+---+---+---+---+---+
  1   2   3   4   5   6   7   8   9   10  11  12  13

+--------+--------+--------+--------+
    1        2        3        4        5

+-----------+-----------+
      1           2           3
```

Timing #10   **After the Report is Written**

12	4	2	Once the report is written, the writer would do well to
24	8	5	forget about the report temporarily. If corrections and
37	12	7	improvements are attempted as soon as the report is finished, the
49	16	10	writer's memory of what was intended may be so strong that the
61	20	12	shortcomings of what was actually written may be overlooked.

12	24	15	When the report becomes fresh to the writer again and
25	29	17	revisions are begun, the following questions should be asked: Is
37	33	20	the report fair, balanced, and clear? Has enough imagination
49	37	22	been used in presenting the facts? Have all the pertinent
62	41	25	questions that might be asked by a reader been answered? Does
74	45	27	the report read as if it were written by a human being? Am I
81	47	28	proud to claim ownership of the report?

12	51	31	This is not the time to be bashful or to worry about how
25	56	33	others might judge your work. If you have peers who are able and
37	60	36	willing to provide a critique of the report, take advantage of
50	64	38	their willingness. Their review will help identify places where
62	68	41	greater clarity is needed or where mechanical errors occurred,
75	72	43	thus interfering with the impact of the report. Be grateful for
87	76	46	all suggestions made. Not all need to be accepted, of course;
--	81	49	but be sensitive to methods by which the writing can be improved.

13	85	51	Writing a report is not a simple accomplishment, especially
25	89	54	if the writer is concerned about quality. The person who can
38	94	56	write clearly, concisely, directly, and with distinction, is a
51	98	59	person whose future in business is bright. If, in addition, that
63	102	61	person can add such factors as excitement, insight, and dramatic
72	105	63	quality, many more career options will open.

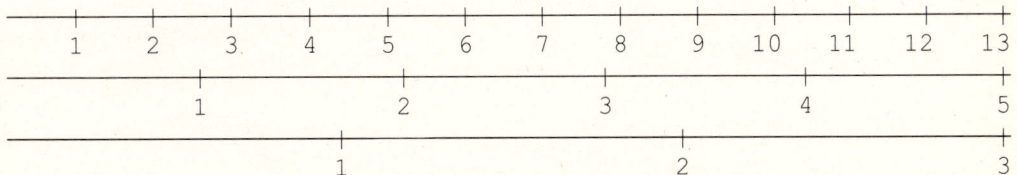

```
    +---+---+---+---+---+---+---+---+---+---+---+---+---+
      1   2   3   4   5   6   7   8   9  10  11  12  13
    +-------+-------+-------+-------+-------+
        1       2       3       4       5
    +-----------+-----------+-----------+
          1           2           3
```

CHAPTER 7

Creating and Editing Applications with WordPerfect 5.1

Lesson 29   Editing Documents with WordPerfect 5.1

Now that you have become familiar with a computer keyboard, it is time to introduce some techniques and tools for editing your work.

We recommend that you keyboard and edit your work at different times—editing requires a set of skills separate from keyboarding.

One editing method is to print a draft, take a break, and then edit the draft with a pencil. Although it is convenient to edit a document on the computer screen, editing tends to be more accurate on a printed document than on a computer. Some people even go to another physical location to do their editing.

Some documents are more difficult to edit than others. For example, if you create a document that contains many numbers, you may want to ask someone to read the document while you read the correct numbers aloud. If there are columns of numbers, a technique to use is to place a ruler under the line of numbers. And if the numbers are extremely complex, instead of reading them in the order intended, read them in reverse order. Each of these techniques can help you to find errors that you may not otherwise find.

If you are unsure about the necessary style, correct word usage, or proper punctuation, you may find it helpful to check an English-language reference book. Three excellent reference books are as follows:

Gibaldi, Joseph, and Walter S. Achtert. *Modern Language Association Handbook for Writers of Research Papers.* 3d ed. New York: Modern Language Association of New York, 1988.

Turabian, Kate L. *A Manual for Writers of Term Papers, Theses, and Dissertations.* 5th ed. Chicago: University of Chicago Press, 1987.

The Chicago Manual of Style. 13th ed. Chicago: University of Chicago Press, 1982.

When correcting rough drafts, you should be familiar with the standard set of editing marks in case others will be keyboarding your corrections. Table 29.1 shows how to use these symbols.

Once you have marked errors or corrections, you can then use WordPerfect 5.1's editing tools to finish the document. You are already familiar with three of the most useful tools: the [Backspace] key, the [Del] key, and the cancel key. Let's look at these keys in more detail.

Using the Backspace Key
[Backspace]

The [Backspace] key is usually above the [Enter] key. It erases the character to the immediate left of the cursor. If characters appear to the right of the cursor, the blank space is filled in because the characters move to the left.

Using the Delete Key
[Del]

As shown in Figure 29.1, a regular keyboard has one [Del] key, and the enhanced keyboard has two.

The [Del] key deletes any character on which the cursor is placed. If you continue to hold down the [Del] key, it will *delete* the text to the right of the cursor one character at a time.

FIGURE 29.1 *An enhanced keyboard has two [Del] keys.*

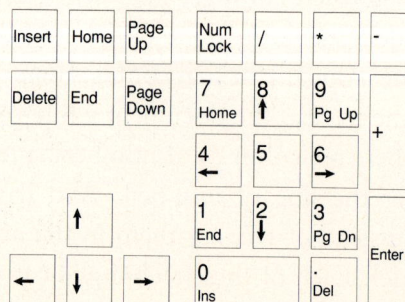

TABLE 29.1 *Editing Marks*

Mark		Draft	Final
∧	caret; insert	is a good	is a very good
◡	close up	some one else	someone else
Caps or ≡	capitalize	Atlantic city	Atlantic City
¶	new paragraph	you there. ¶ Thank you for	you there. Thank you for
⌐	move to left	$45.50 ⌐ 15.95	$45.50 15.95
⌐	move to right	1. Compose 2. Type	1. Compose 2. Type
TR or ∿	transpose	recieved	received
ℯ	delete; take out	We eagerly await	We await
Stet and	leave it as it was originally	last Friday Thursday	last Friday
lc or /	lower case-- not capitalized	her Alma Mater	her alma mater
#	add a space	Thankyou	Thank you
○	spell out	5 files	five files
sp	misspelled word	accuratly done	accurately done
/w	change letter	hole in the hall	hole in the wall
SS	single space	Proofread your work SS before removing it	Proofread your work before removing it
ds	double space	Proofread your work before removing it	Proofread your work before removing it
ts	triple space	ts PROOFREADING Proofread your work	PROOFREADING Proofread your work

If you use the [Del] key on the numeric keypad of an enhanced keyboard, be aware that you need to turn [NumLock] off; otherwise, the numeric key pad is active and the [Del] key enters a period rather than deleting a character. To turn [NumLock] off, press the [NumLock] key once.

Using the Cancel Key (Undelete)
[F1]

With all the editing changes that you will be making to documents, perhaps the most useful key in WordPerfect is the *cancel key* ([F1]). If you delete text by accident, the cancel key, sometimes called the *undelete key*, allows you to get it back—no matter how much text you may have deleted with a command. To see how the cancel key "undeletes" text, follow these steps:

1. Keyboard this paragraph, using word wrap:

   ```
   Good design and interesting, attention-getting
   exhibits are more a matter of common sense,
   creativity, and brilliance than of spending great
   amounts of money.
   ```

   NOTE: Your line endings may vary.

2. Using the cursor arrow keys ([↑], [↓], [→], [←]), move the cursor to the **G** in the word **Good**.

3. Press the [Del] key four times to delete the word.
   RESULT: Each time you press [Del], the character is erased and the remaining text fills in the space.

4. Press the cancel key ([F1])
   RESULT: The word appears on the screen. Depending upon your computer display, the word may appear in a different color or it may appear highlighted. At the bottom of the screen, this prompt appears:
   Undelete: 1 Restore; 2 Previous Deletion: 0

5. Keyboard 1 to restore the text to the screen.
   RESULT: The word **Good** remains on the screen, and you can now move the cursor.

As you can see, using the cancel key to restore text is a two-step process. If you forget to press 1 to restore the text and you press another key, the text will disappear from the screen. But don't worry, just press the cancel key ([F1]) again to get it back. Then be sure to keyboard 1.

In addition to providing tools to erase and recover text, WordPerfect 5.1 also provides tools to help you change existing text. Two of the most important are the insert mode and the Block command ([Alt]-[F4]).

What Is Insert Mode?

With WordPerfect 5.1, you can easily *insert* new text anywhere in the document and the computer will reformat the text for you. You can insert a character within a word, a word within a sentence, or a sentence within a paragraph. To see how WordPerfect 5.1 helps you insert text, follow these steps:

1. Using the cursor arrow keys (↑, ↓, →, ←), move the cursor to the **b** in the word **brilliance** in the paragraph you just keyboarded.

2. Press the Del key ten times to delete the word.

3. Keyboard **ingenuity**.
   RESULT: WordPerfect 5.1 inserts the new text into the paragraph. You can also edit existing text with the Block command (Alt-F4).

Using the Block Command to Bold or Underline Existing Text

So far, you have learned how to bold or underline text as you enter it. However, how do you bold or underline text that you have already keyboarded?

To edit existing text, you first mark it with the *Block command* (Alt-F4). Once text is marked, you can bold it (F6) or underline it (F8). For example, to bold the phrase **attention-getting exhibits** in the paragraph you keyboarded, follow these steps:

1. Move the cursor to the **a** in **attention**.

2. Use the Block command (Alt-F4).
   RESULT: The following prompt starts flashing at the bottom of the screen:

   Block On

3. Move the cursor to the end of the phrase **attention-getting exhibits** by pressing the right arrow key (→) several times.
   RESULT: Depending on the kind of computer display you are using, the marked text either appears in a different color or appears highlighted, as shown in Figure 29.2.

4. Press the Bold key (F6).
   RESULT: The marking disappears and the phrase is bolded.

5. Exit the program by pressing the Exit key (F7) and keyboarding **N** and **Y** to leave the program.
   By using the Del and Backspace keys, along with WordPerfect 5.1's ability to insert and change text, you can make any editing improvements that you like.

```
Good design and interesting attention getting exhibits are more a
matter of common sense, creativity, and ingenuity than of spending
great amounts of money.




















Block on                                    Doc 1 Pg 1 Ln 1" Pos 6.4"
```

FIGURE 29.2

Blocked text either appears in a different color, or appears highlighted on the screen.

Practice 1

Starting WordPerfect 5.1

1. Start WordPerfect 5.1.
2. Place your data disk in drive B, if it is not already there.
3. Keyboard this paragraph *exactly as shown*:

```
Thank yu for sending Exhibit Place your resume.  We were quite
immprsessed by your obvious qualifications and hope you will
visit our offices and fill out an application.  I have pencilled
you in for an interview with Michelle Strongman, Administrative
Manger, on Wedesday, May 22, at 1 p.m.
```

Saving the Lesson

To save the lesson, follow these steps:

1. Press the Save key (F10).
2. Keyboard the name B:LESS29A, then press Enter.

Printing and Editing the Lesson

To print and edit the lesson, follow these steps:

1. Use the Print command (Shift-F7).
2. Keyboard 1 to print the document.
3. Proofread the paragraph.
   a. Keyboard any editing corrections that may be required.

      b. Delete **Wednesday, May 22, at 1 p.m.**, and insert **Friday, May 24, at 10 a.m.**

      c. Resave, replace, and reprint the paragraph.

Exiting WordPerfect 5.1

To end the program, follow these steps:

1. Press the Exit key (F7).
2. Keyboard **N**. You have already saved the document.
3. Keyboard **Y** to leave the program.

Practice 2

Starting WordPerfect 5.1

1. Start WordPerfect 5.1.
2. Place your data disk in drive B, if it is not already there.
3. Keyboard this paragraph *exactly as shown*. Use word wrap. Line endings may vary.

```
    Diligence is the key to becoming a good proofreader.  Using
proofreader's marks, you need to go over materially carefully
marking every error you can find.  In addition use reference
books to check each one of your uncertainties.  Spelling errorsare
often the easier to catch.  Punctuation's errors are usually more
difficult.  Errors in structure of the sentence are the sentence
are the most difficult.
```

Saving the Lesson

To save the lesson, follow these steps:

1. Press the Save key (F10).
2. Keyboard the name B:LESS29B, then press Enter.

Printing and Editing the Lesson

To print and edit the lesson, follow these steps:

1. Use the Print command (Shift-F7).
2. Keyboard **1** to print the document.
3. Proofread the paragraph.
   a. Keyboard any editing corrections that may be required.
   b. Underline every occurrence of the word **proofreader**.

c. Bold every occurrence of the phrase **reference books**.

d. Resave, replace, and reprint the paragraph.

Exiting
WordPerfect 5.1

To end the program, follow these steps:

1. Press the Exit key ([F7]).
2. Keyboard **N**. You have already saved the document.
3. Keyboard **Y** to leave the program.

Practice 3

Starting
WordPerfect 5.1

1. Start WordPerfect 5.1.
2. Place your data disk in drive B, if it is not already there.
3. Keyboard this paragraph exactly as shown. Use word wrap. Line endings may vary.

```
Proofreading is often neglected.  Although it is a extremely
important setp it is too often rushed.  It is quite comon to
allow little of any time for for proofreading with the results
ofthis ommission being all to obvious.  When you are keying
materials especially reports and letters start by proofreading
too often working professionals fel they can make corrections as
they key material.  Although some very experienced writers with
excellent english skills might be able todo this most people must
need to mark in the corrections first so that errors are not
missed.
```

Saving the Lesson

To save the lesson, follow these steps:

1. Press the Save key ([F10]).
2. Keyboard the name B:LESS29C, then press [Enter].

Printing and
Editing the Lesson

To print and edit the lesson, follow these steps:

1. Use the Print command ([Shift]-[F7]).
2. Keyboard **1** to print the document.
3. Proofread the paragraph.
   a. Keyboard any editing corrections that may be required.

b. Bold every occurrence of the word **proofreading**.

c. Underline every occurrence of the phrase **working professionals**.

d. Resave, replace, and reprint the paragraph.

Exiting WordPerfect 5.1

To end the program, follow these steps:

1. Press the Exit key (F7).

2. Keyboard **N**. You have already saved the document.

3. Keyboard **Y** to leave the program.

Review

1. True or False: The Backspace key erases text to the left of the cursor.

2. To erase a character on which the cursor is placed, press the

    _____.

3. True or False: WordPerfect 5.1 automatically reformats a paragraph for you after you have inserted new text.

4. The keystroke(s) to start the Block command is/are _____.

5. The keystroke(s) to restore text that you accidentally deleted is/are

    _____.

6. Mark the appropriate techniques for proofreading documents:

    a. Read the draft on the screen and edit it.

    b. Edit the document immediately, as you create it.

    c. Print the document before you edit it.

    d. Read numbers in reverse order.

Key to Proofreading Practice

Practice 1

```
Thank you for sending Exhibit Place your resume.  We were quite
impressed by your obvious qualifications and hope you will visit
our offices and fill out an application form.  I have penciled
you in for an interview with Michelle Strongman, Administrative
Manager, on Friday, May 24, at 10 a.m.
```

Practice 2

```
Diligence is the key to becoming a good proofreader.  Using
proofreaders' marks, you need to go over material carefully,
marking every error you can find.  In addition, use reference
```

books to check each one of your uncertainties. Spelling errors are often the easiest to catch. Punctuation errors are usually more difficult. Errors in sentence structure are the most difficult.

Practice 3

Proofreading is often neglected. Although it is an extremely important step, it is too often rushed. It is quite common to allow little, if any, time for **proofreading**, with the results of this omission being all too obvious.

When you are keying materials, especially reports and letters, start by **proofreading**. Too often working professionals feel they can make corrections as they key material. Although some very experienced writers with excellent English skills might be able to do this, most people need to mark in the corrections first so that errors are not missed.

Lesson 30   Keyboarding Macros

As you are aware, WordPerfect 5.1 is application software for word processing. Many computer applications, such as WordPerfect 5.1 and Lotus 1-2-3, let you create instructions to communicate in detail with the program. At times you may find that you need to write computer instructions—called macros—that perform routine tasks requiring many keystrokes, such as creating the heading to a memo, keyboarding the closing to a letter, or saving a file. Using a macro, you can do in two keystrokes what normally might take thirty or more.

In this lesson, you will practice writing macros for WordPerfect 5.1 and for Lotus 1-2-3, a popular spreadsheet program.

Practice 1

Starting WordPerfect 5.1

1. Start WordPerfect 5.1.
2. Place your data disk in drive B, if it is not already there.
3. Keyboard the following Lotus 1-2-3 macro. Because the { and } appear in various places on keyboards, strike them in a way convenient for you.
   NOTE: Use the spacebar to space the items in columns, rather than using tabs. Use your judgment in placing the items.

```
Options Menu by Regena Mitchell
April 3, 1990

This Lotus 1-2-3 macro (\O) displays six choices: Display Date,
Format Currency, Save File, Turn Undo On and Off, and Quit.

{MENUBRANCH OPTIONS}
DATE        CURRENCY         SAVE       UNDO OFF   UNDO ON   QUIT
Display     Format Currency  Save File  Disable    Enable
{DATE}      {CURRENCY}       {SAVE}     {UNDO_OFF}{UNDO_ON}  {QUIT}

{PANELOFF}{WINDOWSOFF}                  DATE MACRO
/RFD1~                                  Formats date
@NOW{CALC}~                             Enters date value
/WCS10~                                 Widens column to 10
{WINDOWSON}{PANELON}


/RFC~{?}~                               Formats as Currency

{PANELOFF}{WINDOWSOFF}                  Saves a file
/FS~R
{WINDOWSON}{PANELON}


{PANELOFF}{WINDOWSOFF}                  Disables Undo
/WGDOUDQ
{WINDOWSON}{PANELON}


{PANELOFF}{WINDOWSOFF}                  Enables Undo
/WGDOUEQ
{WINDOWSON}{PANELON}
```

When you have finished, proofread the macro carefully to be certain that every space, punctuation mark, and character has been keyed correctly. Any error, no matter how insignificant, will prevent Lotus 1-2-3 from following the directions intended in the macro.

Saving the Lesson

To save the lesson, follow these steps:

1. Press the Save key ([F10]).
2. Keyboard the name B:LESS30A, then press [Enter].

Printing the Lesson

To print the lesson, follow these steps:

1. Use the Print command ([Shift]-[F7]).
2. Keyboard 1 to print the document.

**Exiting
WordPerfect 5.1**

To end the program, follow these steps:

1. Press the Exit key (F7).
2. Keyboard **N**. You have already saved the document.
3. Keyboard **Y** to leave the program.

Practice 2

**Starting
WordPerfect 5.1**

1. Start WordPerfect 5.1.
2. Place your data disk in drive B, if it is not already there.
3. Keyboard the following WordPerfect 5.1 macro. This macro automatically enters a memo heading in a document. Because the { and } appear in various places on keyboards, strike them in a way convenient for you.

```
{DISPLAY OFF}{Format}18t1{Del to EOL}18{Enter}20{Enter}
{Exit}{Exit}{Tab}TO:{Enter}
{Enter}
{Tab}FROM:{Enter}
{Enter}
TAB{Backspace}{Backspace}{Backspace}{Tab}DATE:
{Date/Outline}t{Enter}
{Enter}
{Enter}
{Tab}SUBJECT:{Enter}
{Enter}
{Enter}
{Format}1L8{Format}LT{Del to EOL}0,5{Enter}
{Exit}{Exit}
```

When you have finished, proofread the macro carefully to be certain that every space, punctuation mark, and character has been keyed correctly. Any error, no matter how insignificant, will prevent WordPerfect 5.1 from following the directions intended in the macro.

Saving the Lesson

To save the lesson, follow these steps:

1. Press the Save key (F10).
2. Keyboard the name B:LESS30B, then press Enter .

Printing the Lesson

To print the lesson, follow these steps:

1. Use the Print command (⌗Shift⌗-⌗F7⌗).
2. Keyboard **1** to print the document.

Exiting WordPerfect 5.1

To end the program, follow these steps:

1. Press the Exit key (⌗F7⌗).
2. Keyboard **N**. You have already saved the document.
3. Keyboard **Y** to leave the program.

Lesson 31

Keyboarding Letters with WordPerfect 5.1

Creating a letter is one of the most common uses for WordPerfect 5.1. In this section, you will learn two formats for business letters: the full block letter and the modified block letter.

The full block letter, shown in Figure 31.1, is popular because it is easy and quick to create. Note that all lines start at the left margin—there are no tabs.

The modified block letter shown in Figure 31.2 was the most common format in business for many years. Although this format is less popular now, many business professionals still feel that indenting the date and the closing makes a letter more attractive.

No matter what the style, a business letter normally contains nine elements:

1. Letterhead
2. Date
3. Inside Address
4. Greeting
5. Body
6. Closing
7. Your name and title
8. Enclosure notation, if you are including something with the letter
9. Carbon copy notation, if more than one person is receiving the letter
   Each of these elements is labeled in Figures 31.1 and 31.2. You will now practice keyboarding letters, using both letter styles.

FIGURE 31.1 *This is an example of the full block letter style.*

(1)

EXHIBIT PLACE
1611 N.W. 12th Avenue
Computer City, CA 94584
(714)555-8107

(2) September 21, 19--

[6-10 returns]

(3) Ms. Ann Konn
5902 Franklin Avenue
Los Angeles, CA 90028

(4) Dear Ms. Konn:

(5) We've seen it happen so many times. A company invests money with a trade show important to its economic growth only to find that to compete, it must spend far more money on exhibits and advertising than it really can afford. After all, it doesn't want to look inferior to other exhibitors.

Perhaps we can help. To compete successfully at the New Wave trade show you do not have to spend several hundred thousand dollars. We have built our reputation on the fact that good design and interesting, attention-getting exhibits are more a matter of common sense, creativity, and ingenuity than of great amounts of money.

AS A PARTICIPANT OF THE NEW WAVE TRADE SHOW, you are guaranteed immediate priority for a Stage A marketing analysis performed by our professional staff. You will not be turned down.

Please read the enclosed material immediately. It provides complete details on how you can take advantage of this exclusive offer.

And remember . . . our immediate analysis is guaranteed.

(DS)
(6) Sincerely,

[2-6 returns]

(7) Patti Gonda
(SS) Customer Representative

(8) Enclosure

(9) cc: Regena Mitchell

FIGURE 31.2 *This is an example of the modified block letter style.*

(1)

EXHIBIT PLACE
1611 N.W. 12th Avenue
Computer City, CA 94584
(714)555-8107

(2)
                                            September 21, 19--

[6-10 returns]

(3)   Ms. Ann Konn
       5902 Franklin Avenue
       Los Angeles, CA 90028

(4)   Dear Ms. Konn:

(5)   We've seen it happen so many times. A company invests money with
       a trade show important to its economic growth only to find that to
       compete, it must spend far more money on exhibits and advertising
       than it really can afford. After all, it doesn't want to look
       inferior to other exhibitors.

       Perhaps we can help. To compete successfully at the New Wave
       trade show you do not have to spend several hundred thousand
       dollars. We have built our reputation on the fact that good
       design and interesting, attention-getting exhibits are more a
       matter of common sense, creativity, and ingenuity than of great
       amounts of money.

       AS A PARTICIPANT OF THE NEW WAVE TRADE SHOW, you are guaranteed
       immediate priority for a Stage A marketing analysis performed by
       our professional staff. You will not be turned down.

       Please read the enclosed material immediately. It provides
       complete details on how you can take advantage of this exclusive
       offer.

       And remember . . . our immediate analysis is guaranteed.
(DS)
(6)   Sincerely,

       [2-6 returns]

(7)   Patti Gonda
(SS)   Customer Representative

(8)   Enclosure

(9)   cc: Regena Mitchell

Practice 1

Starting
WordPerfect 5.1

1. Start WordPerfect 5.1.
2. Place your data disk in drive B, if it is not already there.
3. Keyboard the following letter in modified block form.
   a. To center a line, refer to Lesson 17.
   b. To indent a paragraph, refer to Lesson 18.
   c. Be sure to bold the letterhead by using the Bold key (F6).
   d. Proofread and correct all errors.
   NOTE: Line endings may vary.

Exhibit Place
1611 N.W. 12th Avenue
Computer City, CA 94584

                                    September 12, 19--

Mr. John Erich
354 N. First Street
Computer City, CA 94584

Dear Mr. Erich:

We are sending you a brochure describing what Exhibit Place can
do for you. As explained in the brochure, we have built our
twenty-five-year-old reputation on this simple idea:

    Good design and interesting, attention-getting exhibits are
    more a matter of common sense, creativity, and ingenuity
    than of spending great amounts of money.

We appreciate your interest in Exhibit Place and its activities.
We look forward to answering any of your future inquiries.

                        Sincerely,

                        Ellen Nasus
                        Marketing Director

Enclosure

Saving the Lesson

To save the lesson, follow these steps:

1. Press the Save key (F10).
2. Keyboard the name B:LESS31A, then press Enter.

Printing the Lesson

To print the lesson, follow these steps:

1. Use the Print command (Shift - F7).
2. Keyboard **1** to print the document.

Exiting WordPerfect 5.1

To end the program, follow these steps:

1. Press the Exit key (F7).
2. Keyboard **N**. You have already saved the document.
3. Keyboard **Y** to leave the program.

Practice 2

Starting WordPerfect 5.1

1. Start WordPerfect 5.1.
2. Place your data disk in drive B, if it is not already there.
3. Keyboard the following letter in full block form.
   a. To center a line, refer to Lesson 17.
   b. Be sure to bold the letterhead by using the Bold key (F6) and to underline the appropriate text by using the Underline key (F8).
   c. Proofread and correct all errors.
   NOTE: Line endings may vary.

```
                        Exhibit Place
                  1611 N.W. 12th Avenue
                  Computer City, CA 94584



December 12, 19--



Mr. Ted Nelson
United Technologies, Inc.
125 Mill Street, Suite A
Minneapolis, MN 45943

Dear Mr. Nelson:

Just a reminder that we have an appointment to meet on Monday,
August 5, at 9:00 a.m.  At that time, we will be able to thoroughly
explore how we can provide you with the exhibit that you desire.

Please think about any questions you may have about our services.
I am enclosing some information that will help you formulate your
questions and that will show you how our services compare with
those of our competitors.

See you soon.

Sincerely,



Ellen Nasus
Marketing Director
```

Saving the Lesson

To save the lesson, follow these steps:

1. Press the Save key (`F10`).
2. Keyboard the name B:LESS31B, then press `Enter`.

Printing the Lesson

To print the lesson, follow these steps:

1. Use the Print command (`Shift`-`F7`).
2. Keyboard 1 to print the document.

Exiting
WordPerfect 5.1

To end the program, follow these steps:

1. Press the Exit key (F7).
2. Keyboard **N**. You have already saved the document.
3. Keyboard **Y** to leave the program.

Practice 3

Starting
WordPerfect 5.1

1. Start WordPerfect 5.1.
2. Place your data disk in drive B, if it is not already there.
3. Keyboard the following letter in full block form.
   a. To center a line, refer to Lesson 17.
   b. Be sure to bold the letterhead by using the Bold key (F6).
   c. Proofread and correct all errors.
   NOTE: Line endings may vary.

```
                    Exhibit Place
                 1611 N.W. 12th Avenue
                 Computer City, CA 94584


September 18, 19--


Michael Johnson
President
Horizon Computer Graphics
302 Spring Street, Floor 32
Los Angeles, CA 90264

Dear Mr. Johnson:

I am enclosing change order No. 542910 for you to review and
sign.  By signing and returning the pink copy, you will enable
our builders to make the changes we agreed upon.

Please call me immediately at (302) 555-0493 if this work order
does not reflect our agreed-upon changes.

Sincerely,


Carl Mathews

Enclosure
```

Saving the Lesson

To save the lesson, follow these steps:

1. Press the Save key (F10).
2. Keyboard the name B:LESS31C, then press Enter .

Printing the Lesson

To print the lesson, follow these steps:

1. Use the Print command (Shift - F7).
2. Keyboard 1 to print the document.

Exiting WordPerfect 5.1

To end the program, follow these steps:

1. Press the Exit key (F7).
2. Keyboard N. You have already saved the document.
3. Keyboard Y to leave the program.

Lesson 32   Keyboarding Addresses with WordPerfect 5.1

When the United States Postal Service began using computers to sort envelopes, it became more important than ever to properly address an envelope. Computerized postal systems match street names and ZIP codes on mail with those listed in the postal computer's memory. As a result, street names need to be correctly spelled and ZIP codes need to be accurate to ensure prompt delivery. The ZIP code can be either five digits or nine digits.

The common format for addresses is as follows:

Name
Title
Company
Street Address
City, State, ZIP Code

Usually, the state is abbreviated as two capitalized letters, as shown in Table 32.1, which lists state abbreviations.

Also, if the recipient's title or company name is too long to fit properly in an address, you can place it on two lines and indent the second line two spaces, as follows:

Ms. Deneen Dragonovich
Senior Vice President &
   Chief Financial Officer
Drago Technologies
254 Via Los Miradores
Computer City, CA 94584

Often with WordPerfect 5.1, it is easier to print addresses on mailing
labels than to print envelopes. The reason is that it is easier to print a
large mailing list on labels quickly, and attach them to envelopes, than
to feed envelopes through an electronic printer.

When creating a mailing list with WordPerfect 5.1, keyboard the
addresses so that they print appropriately on labels. Often, three lines
between each address are required.

TABLE 32.1

STATE AND TERRITORY ABBREVIATIONS

AK	Alaska	LA	Louisiana	PA	Pennsylvania
AL	Alabama	MA	Massachusetts	PR	Puerto Rico
AR	Arkansas	MD	Maryland	RI	Rhode Island
AZ	Arizona	ME	Maine	SC	South Carolina
CA	California	MI	Michigan	SD	South Dakota
CO	Colorado	MN	Minnesota	TN	Tennessee
CT	Connecticut	MO	Missouri	TX	Texas
CZ	Canal Zone	MS	Mississippi	UT	Utah
DC	District of Columbia	MT	Montana	VA	Virginia
DE	Delaware	NC	North Carolina	VI	Virgin Islands
FL	Florida	ND	North Dakota	VT	Vermont
GA	Georgia	NE	Nebraska	WA	Washington
GU	Guam	NH	New Hampshire	WI	Wisconsin
HI	Hawaii	NJ	New Jersey	WV	West Virginia
IA	Iowa	NM	New Mexico	WY	Wyoming
ID	Idaho	NV	Nevada		
IL	Illinois	NY	New York		
IN	Indiana	OH	Ohio		
KS	Kansas	OK	Oklahoma		
KY	Kentucky	OR	Oregon		

CANADIAN PROVINCES AND TERRITORY ABBREVIATIONS

AB	Alberta	NS	Nova Scotia
BC	British Columbia	ON	Ontario
LB	Labrador	PE	Prince Edward Island
MB	Manitoba	PQ	Quebec
NB	New Brunswick	SK	Saskatchewan
NF	New Foundland	YT	Yukon Territory

Practice 1

*Starting
WordPerfect 5.1*

1. Start WordPerfect 5.1.
2. Place your data disk in drive B, if it is not already there.
3. Create a mailing list by keyboarding the addresses below. Triple-space between each set of addresses.

```
Ms. Sarah Stevenson
143 Beverly Boulevard
West Los Angeles, CA 91232


Mr. Randy Peynault
23 Elsinor Drive
Seattle, WA 99492


Mr. and Mrs. Fred Wyles
1230 Market Street
San Francisco, CA 94234


Mr. Mike McQuead
P. O. Box 203
Santa Fe, NM 80945


Ms. Rosie Requena
912 Pine Avenue
Boise, ID 73452


Mr. Harry Cohn
President
Atom Software Corp.
355 Chestnut Street
Westwood, NY 07648


Mr. Steven Wharton
Senior Vice-President
Advocate Security Systems
7512 Slate Ridge Boulevard
Columbus, OH 43068


Mr. P. Scott
President
Sciences Assembly Inc.
20 Cross Road
Albany, NY 13224
```

Mr. Ken Hampton
Vice President
Certified Accountants
  Software Company
1211 Avenue of the Americas
New York, NY 10036

Noel Larson
Marketing Director
MicroBound Publishing Company
1412 Fredricks Street
Columbus, OH 54367

Lisa Ohanesian
Northwest Mail Order
120 Seymour Street, Suite 512
Seattle, WA 09745

Mary Oshiro
Marketing Administrator
Computer Interface Specialists
349 Figueroa Street, Suite 1204
Los Angeles, CA 90021

Horace Reginald
President
Reginald Software Games
   and Innovations
Route 1A
Porterville, IN 43256

Ms. Pat Walker
Regional Director
Mercury Software
1702 S. Michigan Street
South Bend, IN 46618

Ms. Judith G. Howard
President
ARCsoft Business Systems
Box 1332
Woodsboro, MD 21798

Mr. Arthur King
President
Atlantis Communications
542 Hallandale Beach Boulevard
Hollywood, FL 33023

Mr. Keith Georgian
Senior Vice President
Digital Network, Inc.
One Penn Plaza
New York, NY 10119

Mr. Bill Birch
Executive President
Baker Circuits, Inc.
511 Forest Lodge Road
Glenn Grove, CA 93959

Mr. John Brahms
Vice President
Computer International Inc.
17110 Lamb Lane
Edina, MN 55435

Mr. Ralph Night
Marketing Director
Cambridge Analysis Co.
32 E. 57 Street
New York, NY 10022

Ms. Michele Farley
Senior Vice President
Career Database Inc.
Box 15486
Orange, CA 92613

Mr. Bill Hickey
President
New Enterprise
Box 1353
Portsmouth, NH 03801

Mr. Larry Baum
President
Baum Associates Inc.
1365 Broadway
Hillsdale, NJ 07642

Mr. James Leaky
President
Leaky, Chimp and Associates
452 Campus Drive, Suite 27
Irvine, CA 92715

LESSON 33 KEYBOARDING A REPORT WITH WORDPERFECT 5.1   147

```
Mr. Bill Lowe
Executive Vice President
National Computing Systems
Box 608
Houston, TX 77252
```

Saving the Lesson

To save the lesson, follow these steps:

1. Press the Save key (F10).
2. Keyboard the name B:LESSON32, then press Enter.

Printing the Lesson

To print the lesson, follow these steps:

1. Use the Print command (Shift-F7).
2. Keyboard **1** to print the document.

Exiting WordPerfect 5.1

To end the program, follow these steps:

1. Press the Exit key (F7).
2. Keyboard **N**. You have already saved the document.
3. Keyboard **Y** to leave the program.

Lesson 33 Keyboarding a Report with WordPerfect 5.1

A report is a business document that involves both research and information gathering. Whether you are a student, businessperson, or government official, you need to know the basics of formatting reports. If your organization uses a format manual, refer to it often. Whatever style you choose, *consistency* is most important so that the readers are not confused by style changes.

There are two types of reports: bound (formal) and unbound (informal). This lesson discusses the unbound report, which is the less formal and shorter of the two. It normally has no cover page or supporting pages, as does the formal report. Headings are usually in this format:

```
               MAIN HEADING OR TITLE

                   (triple space)

              Major Division Headings

                   (triple space)

Side Headings

                   (double space)

Text

                   (triple space)

Side Headings

                   (double space)
```

Remember that when your document is longer than a single page, WordPerfect 5.1 automatically inserts a line of dashes (-) across the screen to show that you are working on a new page.

Practice 1

Starting
WordPerfect 5.1

1. Start WordPerfect 5.1.
2. Place your data disk in drive B, if it is not already there.
3. Keyboard the following informal report.
   a. To center a title, refer to Lesson 17.
   b. To underline text, refer to Lesson 15.
   NOTE: Line endings may vary.

```
               Senses Sell the Product!


All good exhibits stimulate more than one sense at once.  When
working together, sight, sound, touch, smell, and taste are the
best sales tools that we have.
```

MORE ▼

Sight

Simply because a product is small does not mean that it will
"disappear" in an exhibit. You can focus attention upon small
objects by placing them in enclosed spaces. Lighting also plays
an important role in highlighting small objects.

Sound

Sound adds another dimension. Sound and light can set the stage
for any presentation. Department stores use sound and light to
influence customers. Organ music and special lighting may be used
to create a mood to stimulate the sale of religious products.
Carnival music and flashing lights can do the same for the sale of
computer games.

Touch

Don't forget touch when planning an exhibit. Engineers and
technicians love to touch equipment and examine parts minutely.
How about a dial that they can turn or a magnifying glass through
which they can look? Let customers feel the parts of a product.

Smell

The power of association through the sense of smell is a factor
that can be exploited in an exhibit. A scent of pine around a
logging exhibit adds much, as does a scent of roses at a perfume
exhibit. It is a well-known fact that the smell of a new car has
sold many customers.

Taste

Can you develop a strategy to appeal to the taste buds? For
example, a vendor selling a recipe database provided welcome
stations dispensing free orange juice.

Discuss with the clients how all five senses can be used to
enhance their products or services. The sooner clients start
thinking about how all five senses can be used to sell their
products, the more quickly the design process will move.

Saving the Lesson

To save the lesson, follow these steps:

1. Press the Save key (F10).
2. Keyboard the name B:LESS33A, then press Enter.

Printing the Lesson

To print the lesson, follow these steps:

1. Use the Print command (Shift-F7).
2. Keyboard 1 to print the document.

Exiting WordPerfect 5.1

To end the program, follow these steps:

1. Press the Exit key (F7).
2. Keyboard N. You have already saved the document.
3. Keyboard Y to leave the program.

Practice 2

Starting WordPerfect 5.1

1. Start WordPerfect 5.1.
2. Place your data disk in drive B, if it is not already there.
3. Keyboard the following informal report.
   a. To center a title, refer to Lesson 17.
   b. To bold text, refer to Lesson 14.
   c. To underline text, refer to Lesson 15.
   NOTE: Line endings may vary.

WHY USE A PROFESSIONAL EXHIBIT CONTRACTOR?

Trade shows are vital to your company's marketing strategy. At a show, you can generate sales contacts less expensively than by making individual sales calls and you can find many qualified sales prospects. However, simply because you are involved in a trade show does not mean you are developing wise marketing strategies.

Our Services

To prepare you for trade shows, we offer services that include market research, design development, and trade show consulting

MORE ▼

follow-up. In our market research phase, our professional staff
works with your staff to find out your previous show experience.
We teach your staff about each show and the market it reaches.

After completing our Phase A market research analysis, we prepare
press photographs, articles, media kits, and special
advertisements for you. We recommend that you use a direct-mail
program to find qualified and potential customers. We also train
your booth staff in the techniques of selling at trade shows.
Finally, we help you establish a follow-up program for leads using
our direct-mail program.

Phases of Development

Our services are provided to you in three phases:
A. Market Research and Detailed Report (4-6 weeks)
B. Design Development and Production of Exhibit (2-6 months)
C. Trade Show Consulting and Follow-up Services (4-6 months)

Recommendation

It is the professional opinion of Exhibit Place that this program
represents the finest display professionals available for your
industry. For that reason Exhibit Place staff recommends
proceeding to Phase A.

Saving the Lesson

To save the lesson, follow these steps:

1. Press the Save key (F10).
2. Keyboard the name B:LESS33B, then press Enter .

Printing the Lesson

To print the lesson, follow these steps:

1. Use the Print command (Shift - F7).
2. Keyboard 1 to print the document.

Exiting WordPerfect 5.1

To end the program, follow these steps:

1. Press the Exit key (F7).
2. Keyboard N. You have already saved the document.
3. Keyboard Y to leave the program.

Practice 3

Starting
WordPerfect 5.1

1. Start WordPerfect 5.1.
2. Place your data disk in drive B, if it is not already there.
3. Keyboard the following informal report.
   a. To center a title, refer to Lesson 17. To bold text, refer to Lesson 14.
   b. To indent paragraphs, refer to Lesson 18.
   c. To underline text, refer to Lesson 15.
   NOTE: Line endings may vary.

THE BBS BUSINESS PLAN

The Purpose of the BBS

The Exhibit Place Bulletin Board System (BBS) provides customers with information about trade shows in the business environment. Specific services include: product exhibitions, ordering information, and reference material.

Material is organized by industry and by timeliness. Because a bulletin board is most effective when it provides a forum for two-way communication, there is an extensive interactive Question and Answer section.

<u>Benefits</u>

As a central resource for cataloging and accessing related text information, the BBS markets Exhibit Place expertise and professionalism, increases Exhibit Place visibility, and provides staff the opportunity to contribute services that competitors cannot.

<u>Considerations</u>

There are two major issues to address as a result of maintaining a bulletin board with a nationwide access.

1) The BBS is highly visible. Each time a user logs on to the BBS, Exhibit Place's reputation is affected.

MORE ▼

2) Maintaining the BBS requires significant administrative and editorial resources. We estimate that 50% of a professional's time is required as BBS Editor, as well as up to 5-10% of six analysts' time as Area Editors.

Administering the Bulletin Board

The following section details the administrative structure required to maintain the professional quality of the BBS.

Structure

Administering the BBS requires three administrative tiers:
- Six Area Editors
- Exhibit Place supervisors
- Bulletin Board Editor

Writing and Approval Process

Articles are conceived and written in the following manner:

1. Area editor and supervisor agree on article topic.
2. Area editor assigns writer to write the article.
3. Writer may elicit help from BBS editor on writing of article if he or she chooses.
4. Area editor reviews article with writer.
5. Supervisor approves article.
6. BBS editor edits final draft and loads in BBS.

Conclusion

BBS is a highly visible communication tool for Exhibit Place. To maintain credibility, the BBS must consistently present accurate and current information in a professional manner. The BBS must be administered in the same fashion as all our other products.

Saving the Lesson

To save the lesson, follow these steps:
1. Press the Save key (F10).
2. Keyboard the name B:LESS33C, then press Enter.

Printing the Lesson

To print the lesson, follow these steps:
1. Use the Print command (Shift-F7).
2. Keyboard 1 to print the document.

Exiting
WordPerfect 5.1

To end the program, follow these steps:

1. Press the Exit key ($\boxed{\text{F7}}$).
2. Keyboard **N**. You have already saved the document.
3. Keyboard **Y** to leave the program.

Lesson 34   Keyboarding a Resume

The resume is a short, concise, and clear document that advertises what you have to offer an employer. A good resume allows an employer to discover at a glance your accomplishments and what makes you unique and desirable.

There are two major formats for resumes: chronological and functional. A chronological style lists past employment in order by dates, with the most recent experience listed first. The functional resume lists only those experiences that relate to the work you are seeking. Some people have several resumes, each one designed to emphasize specific skills, education, or background.

Practice 1

Starting
WordPerfect 5.1

1. Start WordPerfect 5.1.
2. Place your data disk in drive B, if it is not already there.
3. Keyboard the following resume.
   a. To center a title, refer to Lesson 17.
   b. To bold text, refer to Lesson 14.
   c. To indent paragraphs, refer to Lesson 18.
   d. To underline text, refer to Lesson 15.
   NOTE: Line endings may vary.

Emily Dickerson
2620 Ardmore Street
Computer City, CA 94583
(619) 555-8100

EDUCATION   B.A. Graphics Design
                       University of California, Los Angeles
                       June 1990

EXPERIENCE   <u>Tutorial Assistant</u>
                       Learning and Studies Skills
                       University of California, Los Angeles
                       August 1987 - June 1990

                       Coordinated seven tutors for the campus tutorial
                       program. Developed and managed the tutorial
                       record-keeping system. Designed advertisements
                       for 13 department programs.

                       <u>Administrative Assistant</u>
                       Wilhitte Equipment Dynamics
                       November 1984 - August 1987
                       Prepared invoice and cash-flow reports for
                       management. Coordinated advertising campaign for
                       three products.

SKILLS   IBM Personal Computer: Familiar with Ashton-Tate
                       and RBASE DataBase Management Systems.
                       Experienced with Wordstar, Microsoft Word,
                       WordPerfect, and PageMaker.

REFERENCES   Rachel Howard
                       Art and Design Professor
                       Valley Community College
                       (415) 555-6021.

                       Ray Walker
                       Developmental Editor
                       University of California, Los Angeles
                       (707) 555-8040.

AWARDS   Cy Howard Graphic Design Award First Place
                       University of California, Los Angeles, 1989

Saving the Lesson

To save the lesson, follow these steps:

1. Press the Save key (F10).
2. Keyboard the name B:LESS34A, then press Enter.

Printing the Lesson

To print the lesson, follow these steps:

1. Use the Print command ([Shift]-[F7]).
2. Keyboard **1** to print the document.

Exiting WordPerfect 5.1

To end the program, follow these steps:

1. Press the Exit key ([F7]).
2. Keyboard **N**. You have already saved the document.
3. Keyboard **Y** to leave the program.

Practice 2

Starting WordPerfect 5.1

1. Start WordPerfect 5.1.
2. Place your data disk in drive B, if it is not already there.
3. Keyboard the following resume.
   a. To center a title, refer to Lesson 17.
   b. To bold text, refer to Lesson 14.
   c. To indent paragraphs, refer to Lesson 18.
   NOTE: Line endings may vary.

```
                    Emily Dickerson
                  2620 Ardmore Street
               Computer City, CA 94583
                   (619) 555-8100
```

OBJECTIVE	An entry-level position in graphic design.
EDUCATION	B.A. Graphics Design University of California, Los Angeles June 1990
SKILLS	IBM Personal Computer: Familiar with Ashton-Tate and RBASE DataBase Management Systems. Experienced with Wordstar, Microsoft Word, WordPerfect, and PageMaker.
EXPERIENCE	<u>Tutorial Assistant</u> Learning and Studies Skills University California, Los Angeles August 1987 - June 1990

MORE ▼

<pre>
Designed and developed advertisements, displays,
and brochures for 13 department programs.
Coordinated seven tutors for the campus tutorial
program.

Administrative Assistant
Wilhitte Equipment Dynamics
November 1984 - August 1987

Coordinated advertising campaign in newspaper and
radio for three products.
</pre>

AWARDS
<pre>
Dean's Honor List University of California, Los
Angeles
Cy Howard Graphic Design Award First Place
University of California, Los Angeles, 1990
</pre>

REFERENCES
<pre>
Available upon request.
</pre>

Saving the Lesson

To save the lesson, follow these steps:

1. Press the Save key (F10).
2. Keyboard the name B:LESS34B, then press Enter.

Printing the Lesson

To print the lesson, follow these steps:

1. Use the Print command (Shift-F7).
2. Keyboard 1 to print the document.

Exiting WordPerfect 5.1

To end the program, follow these steps:

1. Press the Exit key (F7).
2. Keyboard N. You have already saved the document.
3. Keyboard Y to leave the program.

A P P E N D I X

A

Using Pull-Down Menus and the Mouse

To help you use WordPerfect 5.1's many features, version 5.1 provides a comprehensive series of pull-down menus containing over 40 word processing commands. These pull-down menus appear across the top of the screen, as shown in Figure A.1.

When a mouse is installed, a solid rectangular pointer (▮) appears on the edit screen and moves as you move the mouse. Activate the pull-down menu system by pressing the right button.

As you can see in Figure A.2, each menu consists of a series of choices. You can select any option by moving the mouse pointer (▮) over a choice and pressing the left button. That's all there is to it. If your mouse has three buttons—as some do—it works the same way: Press the right button to activate the pull-down menu, and press the left button to make

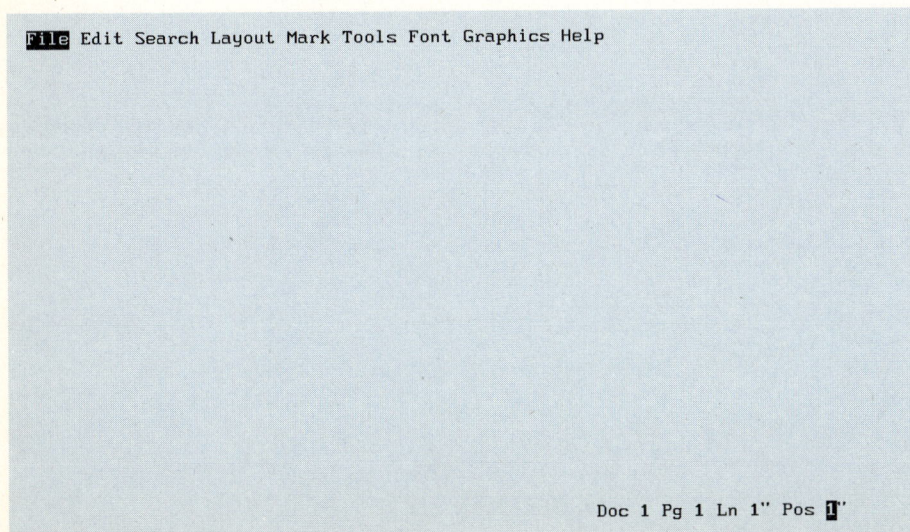

```
File Edit Search Layout Mark Tools Font Graphics Help




















                                        Doc 1 Pg 1 Ln 1" Pos ▮"
```

FIGURE A.I

The nine pull-down menus appear at the top of the screen when you press Alt-=.

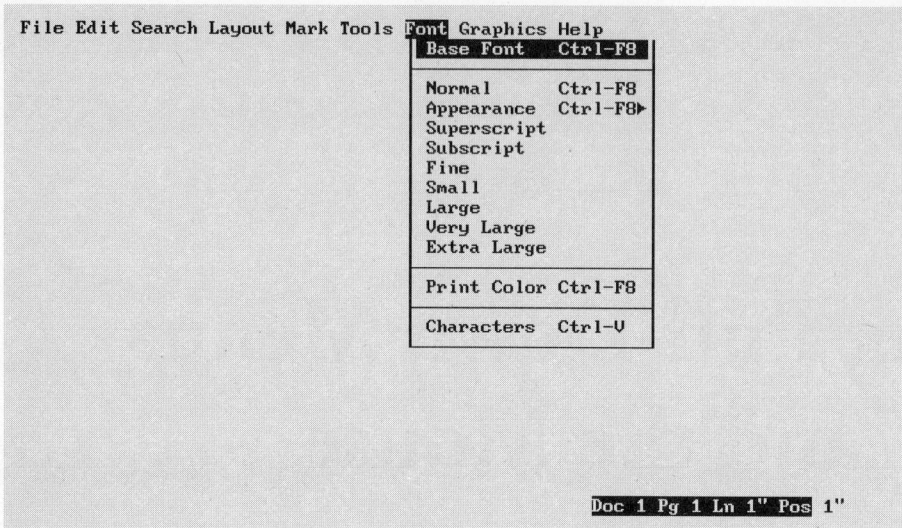

Each pull-down menu consists of a series of choices.

a menu choice. The middle button will cancel any command that you have made.

Have you noticed that next to the Appearance option in Figure A.2 is a solid triangle (➤)? The triangle (➤) means that the item next to it contains a submenu. For example, by selecting **Appearance**, a second-level menu appears, as shown in Figure A.3.

Tables A.1 and A.2 list all the commands used in this book and their associated mouse commands. To use these tables, find the command that you want to perform, and locate the appropriate mouse commands. For example, to underline text, follow these steps:

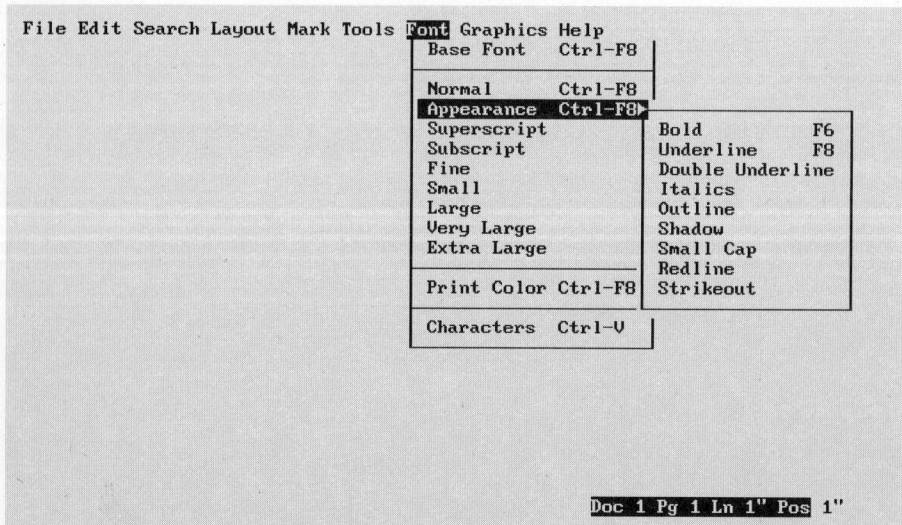

FIGURE A.3

By selecting an option with a triangle (➤) beside it, a second-level menu appears.

TABLE A.I *Using WordPerfect 5.1 Commands with Function Keys and the Mouse*

To Do This Task:	FUNCTION KEY Press:	MOUSE Select:
Bold	F6	Font Appearance Bold
Center	Shift-F6	Layout Justify Center
Change Line Spacing	Shift-F8, 1, 6	Layout Line, 1, 6
Change Tabs	Shift-F8, 1, 8	Layout Line, 1, 8
Exit	F7	File Exit
Indent	F4	Layout Align Indent
Print	Shift-F7	File Print
Save	F10	File Save
Underline	F8	Font Appearance Underline

1. Block the text.
2. Press the right mouse button to activate the pull-down menu.
3. Select the Font option.
   NOTE: When you select Font after blocking text, WordPerfect 5.1 automatically displays the Appearance option for you.
4. Select the Underline option under Appearance. The blocked text is then underlined.
   Using the mouse, you can perform any WordPerfect 5.1 command discussed in this book.

TABLE A.2 *Using the Block Command with a Function Key and a Mouse*

To Block Text	FUNCTION KEY	MOUSE
1.	Move the cursor to the beginning of the text to be blocked.	Move the pointer to the beginning of the text to be blocked.
2.	Use the Alt-F4 command.	Press the left button and hold it down.
3.	Move the cursor to the end of the blocked text.	Move the mouse to the end of the blocked text.

B

Starting WordPerfect on a Two-Floppy-Disk System

If your computer system contains two floppy disk drives (A and B) and no hard disk, you will start WordPerfect by turning on your machine and loading DOS manually. Here are the procedures for doing so:

1. Place your copy of the DOS diskette into the A drive and start your system.

2. Type the current date and press [Enter].

3. Type the date and press [Enter].
   After DOS has been loaded, the disk drive will be silent and its red lights will be off. You should then see the following symbol, called the *A prompt*, on your screen:

   A>

   You are now ready to start WordPerfect. Please be aware, though, that if you learn to start the program from drive B, it will greatly simplify the tasks of saving and retrieving your files. Here's how you do it.

1. Put the data disk in drive B.

2. Type **B:** and press [Enter]. You should see the B prompt on the screen:

   B>

3. Remove the DOS disk.

4. Place the disk labeled WordPerfect 1 into drive A.

5. Type **A:WP** and press [Enter].

Doc 1 Pg 1 Ln 1 Pos 10

FIGURE B.1
The WordPerfect edit screen.

After your computer whirs for a time, you will see this message at the bottom of your screen:

`Insert diskette labeled WordPerfect 2 and press any key`

6. Remove the WordPerfect 1 disk and replace it with WordPerfect 2, and press any key. You should see the screen shown in Figure B.1 and are now ready to begin Chapter 1.

APPENDIX C

Starting WordPerfect on a Hard Disk

If your computer system has a hard disk, it probably has been set up so that you can load DOS just by turning on the computer.

1. Turn on your system.

    What happens next depends on how your computer system has been set up. If you see a menu on your screen, you will have to follow its instructions to start WordPerfect. If you do not see a menu, the following prompt should appear on your screen:

    `C>`

2. Type **WP** and then press ⎡Enter⎤.

    If you see the screen shown in Figure C.1, you have succeeded in starting WordPerfect. Congratulations! You are now ready to start Chapter 1. If you see a message like "Invalid directory" or "Bad command or filename," WordPerfect is probably located in a different directory from the one you are in—or the program is not yet on your hard disk.

3. Type **CD** and press ⎡Enter⎤.

4. Type **DIR *.** and press ⎡Enter⎤.

    RESULT: You will see a listing on your screen of all the files and directories in your root directory. See if you can find a directory that has either WP <DIR>, WP5 <DIR>, or WORD <DIR> in its name. If you do not find one, then contact your instructor, or the person who set up your system. If you do find one, then enter the appropriate command listed in the following table.

FIGURE C.I
*The WordPerfect edit
screen.*

Doc 1 Pg 1 Ln 1 Pos 10

Look For	**Then**
A. WP <DIR>	1. Type **CD\WP** and press [Enter]. 2. Type **WP** and press [Enter].
B. WP5 <DIR>	1. Type **CD\WP5** and press [Enter]. 2. Type **WP** and press [Enter].
C. WORD <DIR>	1. Type **CD\WORD** and press [Enter]. 2. Type **WP** and press [Enter].

You should see the screen shown in Figure C.1 and are now ready to begin
Chapter 1.

D

Performance Graphs

Recording Speed and Accuracy Scores

To see how your performance, speed, and accuracy have improved over time, you may want to record your scores regularly on the Performance Graphs that follow.

To use the graphs follow these steps (see Figure 28.2 for an example of a completed graph):

1. In the **speed** column, put a number in front of the bottom **0** to create a number below which you know your speed will not fall—for example, 20.

2. Record the month and date at the top of the next blank column.

3. Record the length of the timing at the very bottom of the blank column.

4. Place an **S** on the graph in the blank column opposite the GWPM speed obtained on the timing.

5. Place an **E** on the graph in the same column opposite the number of errors obtained on the timing.

6. To make the graph, join the S's from column to column; do the same with the E's.

   Don't worry if your accuracy score fluctuates greatly—accuracy is not a reliable measure. Speed scores, however, should be more consistent, since speed is a highly reliable measure.

PERFORMANCE GRAPH

Name _____   Class _____

Month: __:

Date: __:

Errors	Speed
49	9
48	8
47	7
46	6
45	5
44	4
43	3
42	2
41	1
40	0
39	9
38	8
37	7
36	6
35	5
34	4
33	3
32	2
31	1
30	0
29	9
28	8
27	7
26	6
25	5
24	4
23	3
22	2
21	1
20	0
19	9
18	8
17	7
16	6
15	5
14	4
13	3
12	2
11	1
10	0
9	9
8	8
7	7
6	6
5	5
4	4
3	3
2	2
1	1
0	0

Length of
Timing (in') __:

PERFORMANCE GRAPH

Name _____   Class _____

Month: __:__:__:__:__:__:__:__:__:__:__:__:__:__:__:__:__:__:__:__

Date: __:__:__:__:__:__:__:__:__:__:__:__:__:__:__:__:__:__:__:__

Errors	Speed
49	9
48	8
47	7
46	6
45	5
44	4
43	3
42	2
41	1
40	0
39	9
38	8
37	7
36	6
35	5
34	4
33	3
32	2
31	1
30	0
29	9
28	8
27	7
26	6
25	5
24	4
23	3
22	2
21	1
20	0
19	9
18	8
17	7
16	6
15	5
14	4
13	3
12	2
11	1
10	0
9	9
8	8
7	7
6	6
5	5
4	4
3	3
2	2
1	1
0	0

Length of
Timing (in') __:__:__:__:__:__:__:__:__:__:__:__:__:__:__:__:__:__:__:__

PERFORMANCE GRAPH

Name _____   Class _____

Month: __:

Date: __:

Errors	Speed
49	9
48	8
47	7
46	6
45	5
44	4
43	3
42	2
41	1
40	0
39	9
38	8
37	7
36	6
35	5
34	4
33	3
32	2
31	1
30	0
29	9
28	8
27	7
26	6
25	5
24	4
23	3
22	2
21	1
20	0
19	9
18	8
17	7
16	6
15	5
14	4
13	3
12	2
11	1
10	0
9	9
8	8
7	7
6	6
5	5
4	4
3	3
2	2
1	1
0	0

Length of
Timing (in') __:

PERFORMANCE GRAPH

Name _____   Class _____

Month: ___:___

Date: ___:___

Errors	Speed
49	9
48	8
47	7
46	6
45	5
44	4
43	3
42	2
41	1
40	0
39	9
38	8
37	7
36	6
35	5
34	4
33	3
32	2
31	1
30	0
29	9
28	8
27	7
26	6
25	5
24	4
23	3
22	2
21	1
20	0
19	9
18	8
17	7
16	6
15	5
14	4
13	3
12	2
11	1
10	0
9	9
8	8
7	7
6	6
5	5
4	4
3	3
2	2
1	1
0	0

Length of
Timing (in') ___:___

PERFORMANCE GRAPH

Name _____   Class _____

Month: __:__

Date: __:__

Errors	Speed
49	9
48	8
47	7
46	6
45	5
44	4
43	3
42	2
41	1
40	0
39	9
38	8
37	7
36	6
35	5
34	4
33	3
32	2
31	1
30	0
29	9
28	8
27	7
26	6
25	5
24	4
23	3
22	2
21	1
20	0
19	9
18	8
17	7
16	6
15	5
14	4
13	3
12	2
11	1
10	0
9	9
8	8
7	7
6	6
5	5
4	4
3	3
2	2
1	1
0	0

Length of
Timing (in') __:__

Index

Site Volume Pricing Agreement

WordPerfect Corporation's site volume Pricing Agreement is designed to enable virtually any state-accredited or federally-accredited educational institution, elementary through university, to purchase WPCorp software at prices that correspond with school budgets. Any state- or federally-accredited educational institution needing more than 10 copies of a WPCorp micro computer software product qualifies as a Site.

What is a Site?

A site is considered to be any group of computers that is administrated by one person. A Site can be one classroom, one school, several schools or more. Any changes made to the Site (e.g., adding a minimum of 10 stations, purchasing manuals, updating to a new revision) must be directed through the Site Administrator.

Under the SVPA, the site pays for the initial Master diskettes or Master tape, and an additional price per station (a minimum of 10) which covers the cost of the template, Quick Reference card, and license fee for each station. The site has the option to purchase additional manuals as explained under Additional Manuals.

The Master will be accompanied by a title page stamped with a Grant of Rights. *This title page is the Site's contract with WPCorp and a complete record of the Site purchase.*

Any time changes are made to the Site, this title page needs to accompany the order sent to WPCorp.

Grant of Rights

The accredited educational institution purchasing this package from WordPerfect Corporation may make up to _____ copies of the enclosed master disks for use on institutionally owned or controlled computer workstations only. Copies of these disks may not be taken off the institutional Site for any reason by any person. The educational institution may purchase _____ sets of documentation, of which _____ have already been purchased. To update your Site stations (when future revisions are released), add more stations to your Site, or purchase additional manuals, this title page <u>MUST</u> be returned with the order.

Each time the Site places an order, a new title page with updated information will be returned to the Site.

What are the Prices?

Master Pricing

Includes manual, template, Quick Reference card (if applicable), and software.

	U.S.	Canada†
PC Master*	$75.09	$97.00

*Includes MS/DOS PC machines, Apple IIc/IIe/IIGS, Macintosh, Amiga, and Atari ST. This amount is charged for the first set of Masters and software updates.

†Canadian prices quoted in Canadian dollars. For other Canadian pricing information, call J.B. Marketing at (613) 938-3333 or the WPCorp Orders Department at (800) 321-4566.

Note: Master Prices are quoted for U.S. English versions only. Master Prices for international versions are quoted upon request.

Prices are subject to change without notice or cause.

Per-station software Pricing

Includes license fee, template, and Quick Reference card (if applicable), and software.

Purchase Order Quantity (Not Cumulative)	Price/Station WordPerfect Plan Perfect DataPerfect DrawPerfect WP Office	Price/Station WP-Mac WP-Amiga WP-Atari WP-Executive	Price/Station WP Library WP-Apple IIe/c or IIGS WP Language Modules	Price/Station Int'l Versions
	US/Canada†	US/Canada†	US/Canada†	US/Canada†
10+	$40/$52	$38/$49	$28/$36	$47/$61
20+	$29/$38	$26/$34	$18/$23	$33/$43
30+	$25/$33	$22/$28	$14/$18	$29/$37
100+	$23/$30	$21/$27	$13/$17	$28/$36
500+	$22/$28	$19/$25	$12/$15	$27/$35
1000+	$20/$26	$17/$22	$11/$14	$25/$35
5000+	$19/$25	$16/$21	$10/$13	$24/$31
10000+	$18/$23	$15/$19	$9/$11	$23/$30

†Canadian prices quoted in Canadian dollars. For other Canadian pricing information, call J.B. Marketing at (613) 938-3333 or the WPCorp Orders Department at (800) 321-4566

Prices are subject to change without notice or cause.

Existing Site Updates

A school may update its SVPA Master package for $75. The cost to update its station licenses is $5.00 per station, which includes a newly revised keyboard template and Quick Reference card (if applicable) for each updated station license. Product revisions and updates for VAX, DG, or UNIX products may be obtained by paying an annual subscription fee based upon the type of host machine being used. Contact WPCorp Information Services at (801) 225-5000 for more information.

Individual school-owned packages of WPCorp Software products may be transferred to Site at the time the product is being updated or when additional stations are ordered. Converted stations are under the same restrictions and covenants as any other SVPA station. Contact WPCorp Information Services for further details.

WordPerfect Corporation
1555 N. Technology Way
Orem, Utah 84057
(801) 222-2300
Educational Accounts (801) 222-2300

WordPerfect is getting carried away.

Students and faculty are buying WordPerfect at prices they can't walk away from.

So, if you're a full-time college student, faculty, or staff member, you ought to buy WordPerfect® now. Whether you need WordPerfect for an IBM compatible, Macintosh, Apple, Amiga, or Atari, you can get it for prices far below retail.

Similar discounts are available on PlanPerfect® spreadsheet software, DataPerfect® database management software, and WordPerfect Library.™

To order, simply follow the six steps on the order form below, and sign the agreement to not re-sell or transfer any package purchased under this program. Then send this form to the WordPerfect School Software Program at the address on the right.

WordPerfect
CORPORATION
1555 N. Technology Way · Orem UT 84057
Telephone (801) 225-5000 Telex 820618 FAX (801) 222-4477

— EDUCATIONAL SOFTWARE DIRECT ORDER FORM —

Step 1. Order
Select the appropriate software and disk size for your computer. Please note that you are limited to *one* package of each program.

Product	Price*	Disk Size
☐ WordPerfect 5.1–IBM PC	$135.00	☐ 3½" ☐ 5¼"
☐ WordPerfect 5.1 for OS/2–IBM PC	$150.00	☐ 3½" & 5¼"
☐ WordPerfect 4.2–IBM PC	$125.00	☐ 3½" ☐ 5¼"
☐ WordPerfect–Apple IIe/IIc	$59.00	☐ 3½" & 5¼"
☐ WordPerfect–Apple IIGS	$59.00	☐ 3½"
☐ WordPerfect–Amiga	$89.00	☐ 3½"
☐ WordPerfect–Atari ST	$89.00	☐ 3½"
☐ WordPerfect–Macintosh	$99.00	☐ 3½"
☐ PlanPerfect 5.0–IBM PC	$135.00	☐ 3½" ☐ 5¼"
☐ DataPerfect–IBM PC	$150.00	☐ 3½" & 5¼"
☐ WordPerfect Library–IBM PC	$59.00	☐ 3½" & 5¼"
☐ WordPerfect Executive–IBM PC	$79.00	☐ 3½" & 5¼"

*Prices quoted in U.S. dollars and apply to U.S. delivery for U.S. customers only.

Step 2. Shipping & Handling
Make check or money order payable to WordPerfect for the total cost of the package(s) plus shipping & handling, or complete VISA or MasterCard information below.

# of pkgs	UPS Ground	FedEx 2nd day	FedEx Overnight
1	☐ $ 5.00	☐ $ 8.00	☐ $21.00
2-4	☐ $10.00	☐ $16.00	☐ $30.00
Total	_____		

(Utah residents add 6.25% sales tax)

☐ VISA ☐ MasterCard

Account# _____ Exp. _____

Step 3. Identification
Make a photocopy of your current Student ID or Faculty card *and* a photocopy of some well-known form of identification displaying your social security number, such as your driver's license or social security card. (WPCorp will hold this information strictly confidential and use it only to guard against duplicate purchases.) Your school ID must show current enrollment. (If it does not show a date, you must send verification of current enrollment.) If you have serious reservations about providing a social security number, call the Education Division at (801) 222-1147 to establish clearance to purchase any of the above software products at these special prices.

Step 4. Social Security Number
Enter social security number: ___ ___ ___ – ___ ___ – ___ ___ ___ ___.

Step 5. Address
List your shipping address and the address of the local computer store (dealer) who assisted with this purchase in the space provided (if applicable):

Ship To _____   Dealer of Record _____

_____   _____

_____   _____

Phone _____   Phone _____

Step 6. Sign & Mail
Mail this signed and completed form and your check or money order (or VISA or MasterCard information) to:
School Software Program, WordPerfect Corporation, 1555 N. Technology Way, Orem, UT 84057

I certify that the information provided herein is correct and accurate, that I am a full-time school faculty or staff member, or a full-time post secondary student, and that I will not resell or transfer any package purchased under this program. I understand that at its sole discretion, WPCorp may refuse any order for any reason.

Signature _____ Date _____